**The Actors Fund,
for everyone
in entertainment.**
Celebrating 125 years.

The Actors Fund
is a nationwide human services organization
that helps all professionals in
performing arts and entertainment.
The Fund is a safety net,
providing programs and services
for those who are in need, crisis, or transition.

*Curtain*Call
125 Amazing Years
of
The Actors Fund

THE DONNING COMPANY PUBLISHERS

The Donning Company Publishers
184 Business Park Drive, Suite 206
Virginia Beach, VA 23462

Steve Mull, General Manager
Barbara Buchanan, Office Manager
Pamela Koch, Senior Editor
Amy Thomann, Graphic Designer
Derek Eley, Imaging Artist
Susan Adams, Project Research Coordinator
Scott Rule, Director of Marketing
Tonya Hannink, Marketing Coordinator

Mary Taylor, Project Director for Donning Company Publishers
Celia Gannon, Project Director for The Actors Fund

Library of Congress Cataloging-in-Publication Data
Curtain call : 125 amazing years of the Actors Fund.
    p. cm.
 Includes bibliographical references.
 ISBN 978-1-57864-443-8 (hard cover : alk. paper)
 1. Actors Fund of America--History.
 PN2016.A43C87 2008
 361.7'6--dc22

                                   2007024511

**Printed in the United States of America at Walsworth
Publishing Company**

Contents

Foreword

The Actors Fund, for everyone in entertainment.
Celebrating 125 years.

One hundred twenty-five years is reason to pause and celebrate all the good The Actors Fund has done.

This book chronicles the people who have played important roles in helping us assist our colleagues. It also chronicles the milestones in the life of this unique and inspiring human service organization.

Every image and caption reminds us of how loved The Actors Fund is, especially as seen in the photos of our leaders and scenes from remarkable events. It's important to remember that each image supports the reason for our existence, reminding us of why we were founded and what we do.

The Fund helps seniors and young people, working professionals and those struggling with disability. We assist people in transition that are considering a career change or developing a parallel career. We help people in crisis, whether personal or caused by a catastrophe of nature. In short, we help professionals in entertainment and performing arts who need a helping hand. Today, partnerships with a broad network of caring organizations are critically important and a part of our service. We do so with an eye on the individual in need because that human measure is what matters most.

We are proud of our past and confident that our future will meet the evolving needs of entertainment and performing arts professionals. Enjoy this book, made magnificent by the volunteers and staff that founded, tended, and continue to steward *The Actors Fund for Everyone in Entertainment*.

Joseph P. Benincasa

Joseph P. Benincasa
Executive Director

The Actors Fund wishes to thank...

The Actors Fund Staff; Kevyne Baar; Jay Brady; Veanne Cox; Arthur & Barbara Gelb; Gail Malmgreen; Laurence Maslon; Museum of the City of New York; New York Performing Arts Library; Bebe Neuwirth; Phyllis Newman; Photofest; Steve and Anita Shevett; Jerry Stiller; Tamiment Library/Robert F. Wagner Labor Archives, New York University; Tom Viola; Amy Waters Yarsinske

ACTORS FUND

The Past

GRAN

OPEN
1 to 11
DAILY

MAY 12-21 AD

INCLUDING SUNDAY

INTERIOR of the MADISON SQUARE GARDEN. ACTORS FUND FAIR.

Exits *and* Entrances

By Laurence Maslon

S"Some actors are a *tour de force*," the actress Hermione Gingold once opined, "others are forced to tour." For the first century of their profession, American actors—no matter their skill—were, indeed, forced to tour. But the technology of the cross-country railroads that emerged in the wake of the Civil War would change the face of the American theater forever. Between 1865 and 1880, the miles of railway track crisscrossing the United States had quadrupled—and this allowed for actors of major talent to appear nearly anywhere in the country.

By 1878, almost all touring productions—combination companies they were called—originated in New York. It had become the center of American theater with twenty-eight permanent theaters—more than Philadelphia and Boston combined—and managers, agents, and actors found it convenient and profitable to begin a tour fresh from a New York success. But although New York was the logical locus for combination companies, it was the rigorous schedule of touring on the road that made an actor's fortune. In 1887–88, Edwin Booth and his coproducer/acting partner Lawrence Barrett launched a tour that played 258 performances in seventy-two towns. Often major stars had their own railway coaches—

Maude Adams had her car fitted with scenery so that her company could rehearse while they traveled—but for most of the company, railway travel was arduous. One manager roused his company between 5:30 and 6:00 every morning of their tour to catch a train to the next engagement—even though a later one would have done. They often had to wait in the hotel lobby for other guests to vacate, and avoid the hotels that posted signs, "No Actors or Dogs Allowed." Touring meant irregular hours, uncertain food, and exposure to the elements. Young unmarried actresses on the road were particularly vulnerable, and many an actor turned to alcohol—or even drugs—to relieve the monotony of a life that usually began at 8 o'clock at night—and which ended long after the sleepy towns on tour had gone to bed. Touring required stamina, but as one actor of the period claimed, "Once you are launched, the road possesses a lure, distinct, perennial and gripping."

Still, for an actor in the nineteenth century, a cold and isolated life spent traveling in an anonymous train compartment was largely the norm. Such a life had its compensations, usually the world of applause and the occasional burst of fame, but it could be lonely—and often dangerous. In 1879, a strapping, romantic leading man named Maurice Barrymore was taking his company on a tour of various melodramas and farces through the dusty rural towns in Texas. Barrymore was born in England—one of the last of a breed of nineteenth-century British actors to seek their fame and fortune in America. He was originally named Herbert Blythe but changed his

≡ Maude Adams in the title role of *Rosalind*, one of the many roles rehearsed during railway travel. *Courtesy of the George Grantham Bain Collection, Library of Congress Prints and Photographs Division.*

Actors and managers in New York demanded a boycott of playhouses in Texas; likewise, authorities in Texas blamed the licentious lifestyles of traveling actors for the incident. None of the furor helped Benjamin Porter get buried. He had a widow and children—and certainly no pension fund or stocks and bonds in the bank. His body was shipped back to New York and awaited a proper burial.

For many actors, the final exit was the most difficult one of all. Proper burials for actors were often hard to come by. Many actors, like Barrymore, had changed their names, so family members had long vanished into their pasts. In the nineteenth century, long before the days of social security, pensions, and unions, charity often resided in local church groups—and no single institution was more hostile

name in order not to bring shame upon his family. Following a one-night stand in the small cow town of Marshall, Texas, on the Louisiana border, Barrymore and two of his troupe—an actress named Cummins and an actor named Benjamin Porter—wanted some refreshment after the performance. Only a small saloon was open that night, and a local patron of the establishment—drunk to the gills—started harassing Barrymore and his colleagues. Barrymore had started his career as a boxer—all the while maintaining his handsome profile—and managed to fend off the offensive intruder with the threat of fisticuffs, while Porter and Cummins headed out the swinging doors. But this was a tiny Texas border town, and the drunken man simply resorted to the language best spoken there: he pulled out his revolver and shot Porter in the back.

≡ Maurice Barrymore circa 1880. *Courtesy of the George Grantham Bain Collection, Library of Congress Prints and Photographs Division.*

The life of an actor is a fictitious one, being made up of the personification of other characters, often gross and immoral, even diabolical. It is a subtle law which governs histrionic art that one must have sympathy for the role he plays.

—Reverend Perry Sinks, 1875

to actors than the Church. The Puritan prejudice toward drama was as deeply ingrained in America as in England; it was denounced from the pulpit as early as 1757, a few years after the British Hallam family introduced professional theater to America. Throughout much of the nineteenth century, clerical disdain dissuaded many Americans from attending the theater.

In 1870, the most beloved American actor of the post–Civil War era, Joseph Jefferson, was asked by the widow of a member of his company, George Holland, to arrange for his burial and church service. Holland was also a popular actor with many friends, and Jefferson was the most revered actor of his day, next to Edwin Booth. He called upon the pastor of his neighborhood church in New York and inquired about a church burial service for his friend. The pastor's back stiffened and his eyes grew cold upon hearing that Jefferson's colleague was an actor—and refused to perform the service. Jefferson "felt a mortification that I had not felt before or since. 'Pray tell me,' I asked the pastor, 'is there no church where I can get my friend buried?' 'Well,' he drawled, 'there is that little church around the corner where they do that sort of thing.'"

≡ Joseph Jefferson (1829–1905), photographed between 1860 and 1875, was the third actor of this name in a family of actors and managers, and one of the most famous of all American comedians. He took a substantive, participatory role in The Fund's early Fairs, introducing the 1892 Fair with colleague Edwin Booth. *Courtesy of the Library of Congress Prints and Photographs Division.*

"God bless the little church around the corner," sighed Jefferson, and the Church of the Transfiguration on Fifth Avenue and Twenty-ninth Street gained a new name that continues to this day. It was there that, eight years after Holland's burial, the murdered actor, Benjamin Porter, finally found his resting place.

As Mark Antony says in *Julius Caesar*, "The evil that men do lives after them/the good is oft interred with their bones." So it was with poor Benjamin Porter. The theatrical community was so moved by his plight—and his wife's misfortune—that they staged a series of benefit performances that raised more than

$17,500 for the grieving widow. Apparently, upon receiving the vast sum, her hair grew "quite gold from grief," as Oscar Wilde's Lady Bracknell would have put it. She promptly remarried, made a lot of money in real estate investments, and took off for points unknown.

Benefit performances had long been a theatrical tradition, but, prior to the twentieth century, the combined box office receipts of a benefit performance always went to one individual—usually the leading actor or actress in the company. By the time of Mrs. Porter's quick fortune, the practice had gotten out of hand, with actor-managers calling for benefit performances with alarming frequency. The perceived misuse of benefit funds by Porter's widow incensed the theatrical community. In 1880, the editor of the *New York Dramatic Mirror*—the city's most influential theatrical newspaper—was an eighteen-year-old theater fan named Harrison Grey Fiske. Fiske was a freshman studying at New York University when his father, who had owned the *Mirror*, died, leaving the paper up for grabs. Fiske quit school and moved

≡ The Little Church Around the Corner, officially the Church of the Transfiguration, was built at One East Twenty-ninth Street between Fifth and Madison avenues in 1849. There has been a close association between this church and the theater from 1870, a relationship that fostered the establishment of the Episcopal Actors' Guild in 1923. *Courtesy of the Library of Congress Prints and Photographs Division.*

quickly to try to gain control of the paper and—thanks to a ten-thousand-dollar loan from Edwin Booth—succeeded.

From day one, Fiske became an ardent crusader to change the nature of benefit performances—the box office receipts must cease to line the pockets of one individual, he propounded, and should instead be shared among the theatrical community to protect their own. Fiske proposed a "sinking fund"—a financial resource that could be used by all members of the theatrical profession in times of

≡ Harrison Grey Fiske (1861–1942) was a New York University freshman in 1879 when he took over the *New York Dramatic Mirror*. Almost immediately, he began a concerted campaign for an "actors' fund." Despite his young age, Fiske proved to an influential and powerful group of theater managers that something must be done to guard the welfare of those working in their establishments. By 1882, most theater managers and syndicate owners had become sufficiently interested in the subject to act on Fiske's recommendations. Fiske and his wife, Minnie Maddern Fiske, were both life members of The Actors Fund. *Courtesy of Louis M. Simon's A History of the Actors' Fund.*

need. The contributions would come annually from members of all the theatrical professions. By the time Fiske had taken control of the *Mirror*, there were nearly ten thousand actors spread across the country, and the logistics required to pull together actors, managers, and producers to create—let alone administer—such a general fund were enormous.

But the need was great, and the pressure to create a fund was coming from all sides. In 1881, a touring actress named Eliza Norton had died, and her body was brought back to New York City, where it waited unclaimed by her family and unburied. Even her manager refused to help. Local newspapers were filled with stories about how "the theatrical profession refused to look after its own." For Fiske, this was the last straw; he redoubled his efforts to create a fund, and in March of 1882, he received commitments from several actors to put together a benefit performance where the receipts would go entirely to jumpstart the new Actors Fund. A benefit performance at Haverly's 14th Street Theater on March 12 was a small but organized affair, and a subsequent

≡ The first benefits for The Actors Fund were largely successes because of the consistent stream of editorials written by Harrison Fiske in the *New York Dramatic Mirror*. However, it was actress Fanny Davenport (1850–1898) who ignited the fire that drove the theatrical profession to raise an "actors' fund." The publication of her letter of endorsement in the *Mirror* was influential, but it was her relationship with Fiske that paved the way. *Courtesy of the Library of Congress Prints and Photographs Division.*

≡ Edwin Forrest (1806–1872) earned his notoriety as a tragedian, beginning with his role as Othello on the New York stage in 1826. A native Philadelphian, Forrest was instrumental in the formation of several local theatrical funds and ultimately brought his passion and experience to the formation of The Actors Fund. *Courtesy of the Brady-Handy Collection, Library of Congress Prints and Photographs Division.*

benefit three weeks later raised $17,000. By the end of the month, the brand-new Actors Fund had $35,000 in the till, with $10,000 contributed by James Gordon Bennett, the celebrated editor of the *New York Herald* (he had famously sent Stanley to Africa after Livingstone), plus donations from, among others, Edwin Booth, Buffalo Bill Cody, Macy's Department Store, and James O'Neill, the popular actor and father of Eugene O'Neill. "The astonishing success of the Actors Fund had proved the existence of a striking esprit de corps among the profession," wrote a local newspaper.

The Fund had placed its trust in a revered New York producer named A. M. Palmer to manage its funds, and within a year, the Fund was able to assist four hundred theatrical workers across the country; this included providing proper burial for thirty-two professionals and bringing twelve stranded actors from across the country back to New

≡ Actor and composer Joseph Kline Emmet was among the first to respond to the *New York Dramatic Mirror*'s call for performances to benefit an actors' fund on its January 28, 1882, editorial page. In addition to donating ticket sales, Emmet also made a personal contribution of $1,000. *Courtesy of the Theatrical Poster Collection, Library of Congress Prints and Photographs Division.*

York. Within five years, it had managed to purchase twenty burial plots on a beautiful site in a cemetery in Brooklyn. At the dedication ceremony, Edwin Booth himself spoke about the occasion, and an audience of ten thousand people ventured to the Cemetery of the Evergreens to hear him.

There's not an actor alive who hasn't wished for a round of applause on his or her final exit from the stage. Thanks to the pioneering dreams of Edwin Booth, Joseph Jefferson, and Harrison Grey Fiske, among others, The Actors Fund has seen to it that no actor would have to suffer the indignity of an unacknowledged final exit ever again.

≡ Minnie Maddern Fiske (1865–1932) was one of the best-known stage actresses at the turn of the twentieth century. In 1890, she married playwright and theatrical manager Harrison Grey Fiske. Over the years, she contributed her talents to many benefits for The Fund. *Courtesy of the George Grantham Bain Collection, Library of Congress Prints and Photographs Division.*

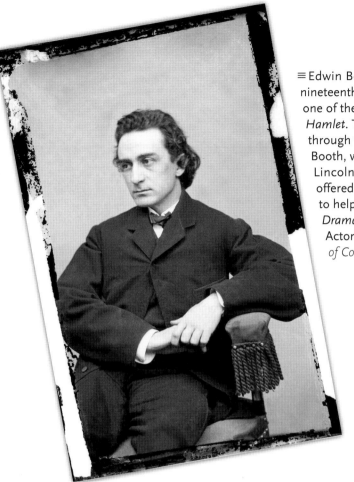

≡ Edwin Booth (1833–1893) was the renowned nineteenth-century tragedian best remembered as one of the greatest performers of Shakespeare's *Hamlet*. The Booth family garnered much fame through the years, although brother John Wilkes Booth, who assassinated President Abraham Lincoln, tainted it. In 1879, Edwin quietly offered a $10,000 loan to Harrison Grey Fiske to help acquire full control of the *New York Dramatic Mirror*. From this partnership, The Actors Fund was born. *Courtesy of the Library of Congress Prints and Photographs Division.*

≡ Phineas Taylor "P. T." Barnum (1810–1891), a founder of The Actors Fund and a member of its original Board of Trustees, was a showman better known outside the theater. His knowledge and expertise were instrumental in coordinating booking operations and publicity. *Courtesy of the Brady-Handy Photograph Collection, Library of Congress Prints and Photographs Division.*

> *"The astonishing success of the Actors Fund had proved the existence of a striking esprit de corps among the profession."*

≡ Albert Palmer (1838–1905) graduated from the Law School of New York University before becoming manager of the Union Square Theatre. His business background made him a natural leader in The Fund's development, holding a series of benefits and securing a charter for the fledgling organization. *Courtesy of the George Grantham Bain Collection, Library of Congress Prints and Photographs Division.*

≡ Colonel William F. "Buffalo Bill" Cody (1846–1917) brought his Wild West show to the cavernous Seventy-first Regiment Armory as part of the 1910 Actors Fund Fair. His relationship to The Fund began in 1882 with a $100 donation, making him a founding contributor. *Courtesy of the Library of Congress Prints and Photographs Division.*

On March 12, 1882, a meeting of the managers of several theaters was held in the office of Albert Palmer's Union Square Theatre. At this meeting, it was decided to officially establish the organization to be known as The Actors Fund. A committee was appointed to "solicit subscriptions and organize a benefit," with another appointed to "permanently organize the Fund and secure a charter." These committees outlined the principles that were later embodied in the formal articles of incorporation. From this meeting, which included Albert Palmer, Lester Wallack, and Daniel Frohman among other top theatrical managers, it was determined that benefits would be held in nearly all the theaters of New York City and Brooklyn.

It is of the utmost significance that the theatrical managers of New York worked together to establish April 3, 1882, as "Actors Fund Day." Never before had the same degree of unanimity been displayed among them. Their coordinated efforts of performances and special individual gifts raised more than $40,000 for the new fund. James Gordon Bennett, John Jacob Astor, J. K. Emmett, Buffalo Bill Cody, and R. H. Macy were just a few of the original contributors. ❧

≡ The Union Square Theatre was the site of the March 12, 1882, meeting that laid the foundation of The Actors Fund. *Courtesy of Tamiment Library/Robert F. Wagner Labor Archives, New York University.*

≡ New York City's famous Union Square, shown here as it appeared around 1882, was home to Albert Palmer's Union Square Theatre. *Courtesy of the George Grantham Bain Collection, Library of Congress Prints and Photographs Division.*

How the Bonding of Actors Gave Birth to The Actors Fund

By Arthur Gelb and Barbara Gelb

*I*n the early spring of 1882, Edwin Booth and James O'Neill were among the prominent players who helped create The Actors Fund to assist their often-impoverished fellow performers.

Booth was America's heralded Shakespearean actor in an era when Shakespeare drew packed audiences in theaters throughout the country. Generous and thoughtful to a fault, Booth habitually encouraged and guided aspiring actors, and was universally loved and admired. His fellow thespians were ever aware of Booth's haunting pain over his brother's assassination of Lincoln a decade earlier—a personal tragedy from which he never recovered.

One such young actor was James O'Neill, whose gift for playing Shakespeare was quickly recognized by Booth. In 1873 and 1874, Booth and O'Neill per-formed in repertory at McVicker's Theater in Chicago to overwhelming audience and critical acclaim. With his unswerving magnanimity toward younger players, Booth offered to alternate with O'Neill in the roles of Iago and Othello.

Toward the close of their first season at McVicker's, O'Neill was described by the *Chicago Daily Times* as "one of the best of the few good leading men in the country." He was already being talked of in theater circles as Booth's likely successor.

O'Neill was forever grateful to his mentor. He later told an interviewer, "Booth was not only the greatest actor without a doubt the world has ever seen, but the noblest man the stage has produced."

Their collegiality during those two McVicker seasons was later recorded for posterity by James's son, Eugene O'Neill, in an emotional speech in *Long Day's Journey into Night*. Theirs was a stage

≡ Edwin Booth (1833–1893), pictured here in Shakespeare's *Hamlet,* shared his generous spirit with the young actor James O'Neill. *Courtesy of the Library of Congress Prints and Photographs Division.*

bonding not uncommon to the touring actors of the nineteenth century.

In those days that knew no radio, film, or television, virtually every American town boasted a playhouse, and actors lived in close proximity (even if not always in perfect harmony) as they trekked from theater to theater—often performing one-night stands—and together confronted untold hardships. It was a grueling—and frequently underpaid—life. More often than not, actors had no choice but to travel in rickety railroad cars that lacked diners and to sleep in shabby hotels.

The hotels did, however, harbor saloons, where cheap liquor was plentiful, and it was there that the touring actors gathered after performances to commiserate and exchange shoptalk—and consolidate their bonds.

prodiciously gifted but unstable and alcoholic. Booth had overcome his own alcoholism after the death of his first wife some ten years earlier. Not long after, his younger brother's assassination of Lincoln had sent him into a year's seclusion.

As for James O'Neill, at twenty-seven, he too had managed to overcome much of the bias toward actors by his talent, charm, and handsome bearing. In 1874, one Chicago newspaper focused on O'Neill's uncanny resemblance to his mentor: "Most of all did he become the pattern of Edwin Booth. So keenly did he study Booth that he copied even his defects in mannerisms. He dressed like him, posed like him, and finally came to speak like him." The transformation was all the more amazing in view of James's early years as the son of an impoverished Irish immigrant family.

The onstage camaraderie between Booth and the younger O'Neill was demonstrated by one particular rehearsal for *Othello* at McVicker's. It also shows the way actors of their day functioned without directors, relying on their own instincts, experience, and technique—and more or less oblivious to the concept of an ensemble performance.

When the actors in *Othello* were running through their roles on the afternoon before the performance, O'Neill conceived the novel bit of business that was to distinguish his Othello. Determined to make his

O'NEILL as ABBE BUSONI
IN
MONTE CRISTO.

≡ James O'Neill (1849–1920), father of playwright Eugene O'Neill, became fast friends with Edwin Booth in 1873 at McVicker's Theater in Chicago. *Courtesy of the Library of Congress Prints and Photographs Division.*

While most actors were regarded as a class apart—women as little better than prostitutes and men as alcoholic riffraff—Edwin Booth was among the rare exceptions. At the age of forty, he was the picture

"It was such bonding among actors on stage—and their concern off stage for one another's welfare in sickness and old age—that led to the remarkable birth of The Actors Fund."

of manly elegance. His personal charm and courtly bearing dazzled playgoers—men as well as women.

Booth wore his dark hair long, and his dark, deep-set eyes glowed in a thin, sensitive face. As a boy, he had toured as guardian to his actor-father, who was

mark with the role, he hit on the idea of wearing an ancient sword he'd picked up during his early barnstorming days; the sword, when he tried backstage to draw it from its ornamented scabbard, came only halfway out and then clanged back.

At the appropriate moment during the actual performance, O'Neill approached Booth's Iago. Menacingly drawing the sword, he spoke the line, "Nay, stay: thou shouldst be honest"—and to the audience's surprise, as well as Booth's, he let go of the sword hilt. The sound reverberated throughout the huge, hushed theater. The audience, so knowledgeable it could be enchanted by even such a minor innovation, nearly fell out of its seats in its effort to applaud O'Neill. Booth called O'Neill back onstage to take extra bows.

"The scene is yours," said Booth. "You couldn't have done it better."

The caring that Booth lavished on his young acolyte was illustrative of the acting craft in general across America in the nineteenth century. It was such bonding among actors on stage—and their concern off stage for one another's welfare in sickness and old age—that led to the remarkable birth of The Actors Fund. ✄

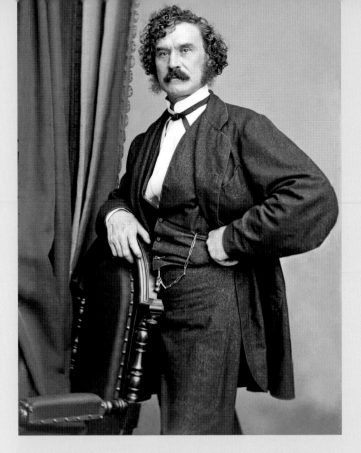

≡ Lester Wallack (1820–1888) was a renowned actor, ultimately finding greater success as a theater manager. He managed Wallack's Theatre from 1861 and, in 1882, offered the space for benefits and meetings for The Actors Fund. Wallack was the first president of The Fund, from 1882 to 1883, and on its Board of Trustees until 1885. *Courtesy of the Library of Congress Prints and Photographs Division.*

The act of incorporation for The Actors Fund was drafted by the Honorable Abram J. Dittenhoefer as special legislation by the New York state legislature and became law on June 8, 1882. The roster of fifty-seven original incorporators read like a who's who of American theater, among them: Lester Wallack, Albert Palmer, Edwin Booth, Edward Harrigan, Joseph Jefferson, Phineas T. Barnum, Dion Boucicault, Daniel and Charles Frohman, and James O'Neill. The word "profession" was defined in the act of incorporation to include all who earn a living in connection with the theater.

The first meeting of the association for the purpose of perfecting its organization under the act of incorporation was held at Wallack's Theatre on

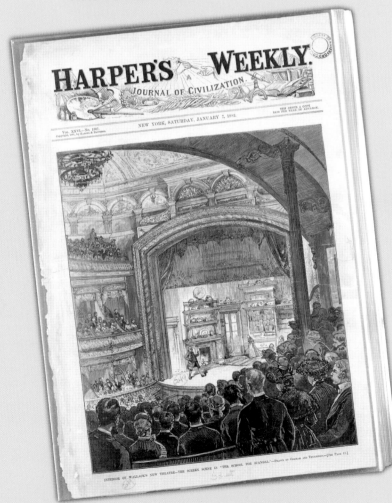

≡ The interior of Wallack's Theatre, shown on the cover of *Harper's Weekly*, was the site of The Fund's first official meeting after the New York state legislature granted the incorporation. *Courtesy of the Library of Congress Prints and Photographs Division.*

them. A section within the Cemetery of the Evergreens in Brooklyn was purchased for $3,600 in 1885. In the late nineteenth and well into the twentieth centuries, it was all too often the case that young men and women in theatrical professions ran away from home, severing ties with their families and their families' finances. If a runaway had not become prominent and death came early, no relative would know of their loved one's demise and claim the body. Thus, the emphasis placed by The Fund's early trustees on a decent burial was not a nicety but a necessity. The section of the Cemetery of the Evergreens contained twenty burial plots, but not wanting to use monies collected "for relief," the trustees stopped short of authorizing payment for a monument that would serve as an appropriate centerpiece for The Fund's part of the cemetery.

They launched, instead, a special drive that netted nearly $6,500. This was substantially more than was required to erect a monument. The surplus was

≡ The jewel-funded obelisk is erected in 1941 at The Actors Fund plot in Kensico Cemetery, Valhalla, New York. *Courtesy of Tamiment Library/Robert F. Wagner Labor Archives, New York University.*

Saturday, July 15, 1882, with William Henderson presiding. This meeting was marked in the records of the association as its first annual meeting, and from this all other subsequent annual meetings are numerically reckoned. At a subsequent meeting held at Wallack's on September 14, 1882, the bylaws of The Fund were prepared in accordance with the official act of incorporation.

The first major capital expenditure approved by the new Fund was inspired by the turbulent struggle between the theatrical community and society's view of

≡ The front page of the June 18, 1887, *Harper's Weekly* featured the dedication of The Actors Fund monument in The Fund's plot at the Cemetery of the Evergreens in Brooklyn. Edwin Booth and Joseph Jefferson spoke at the event, which had over ten thousand people in attendance. *Courtesy of Amy Waters Yarsinske.*

added to general relief funds. On June 6, 1887, an imposing granite obelisk was dedicated during an elaborate ceremony presided over by Edwin Booth, the keynote speaker.

The Cemetery of the Evergreens became the repose of eight hundred notables from the entertainment industry. But Actors Fund trustees realized early on that their plots in the Evergreens had filled all too quickly. The Fund bought a second plot at Kensico Cemetery in Valhalla, Westchester County, New York, in 1904 with jewels. The trustees wanted a monument erected in the cemetery similar to the obelisk at Cemetery of the Evergreens but did not want to use money set aside for care of the sick, aged, and needy to do so. Fund President Walter Vincent remembered that in 1929 Edna McCauley Lewisohn Fox had bequeathed jewelry to The Fund with the proviso that it remain available for the use of her friend, Georgia "Georgie" Caine, a star of the musical theater and talking pictures. Vincent went to Caine to make arrangements to take possession of the jewelry. She cheerfully and generously relinquished all claims to it, turning them over for The Fund's use. But it was 1931, and there was no market for jewelry. The jewelry remained in The Fund's vault until 1940, when it was reappraised and sold to purchase a monument for The Actors Fund plot at Kensico Cemetery. ✍

≡ The Kensico monument. *The Actors Fund Archives.*

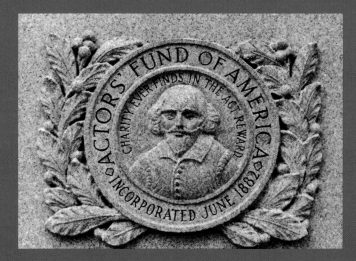

≡ A close-up of the Kensico monument insignia, featuring William Shakespeare. *The Actors Fund Archives.*

The first Actors Fund Fair was held at Madison Square Garden from May 2 to May 7, 1892. Under the direction of renowned architect and decorative arts expert Stanford White, Madison Square Garden was transformed into a fantastic village, giving spectators the look and feel of a world's fair. Albert Palmer, then president of the Fund's Fair Committee, opened the festivities. He made a brief speech, thanking those who had worked so hard to transform the Garden and set up the attractions and then introducing Edwin Booth and Joseph Jefferson. Booth simply bowed, but Jefferson said, "As the name of Shakespeare comes up before me, this being the Actors' Fund, and he the high priest of my profession, may I repeat a few lines of my own?

The wondering world asks what was his profession?
Of course he was a lawyer, says the lawyer,
He must have been a sawyer, says the sawyer,
The corner druggist says he was a chemist,
The skilled mechanic dubs him a great thinker

And every tin man swears he was a tinker,
And so he's claimed by every trade and factor,
Your pardon, gentlemen—he was an actor.

As patrons entered the Garden, they were met with a triumphal arch and Roman colonnade that served as the entrance to a village street. Festive booths lined the walkway, displaying everything from a diamond necklace that was to have been presented as a wedding gift to Prince Albert Victor and Princess May of the British Royal family to three volumes of *Uncle Tom's Cabin*, donated and autographed by Harriet Beecher Stowe.

A commemorative ladle was commissioned for the Fair, with the likeness of five actresses on one side and five actors on the other, while its bowl contained an engraving of the Park Theatre, and the reverse said, "Actors' Fund Fair, May 2 to May 7, 1892." Small spoons with portraits of actresses were also commissioned. There were fifteen actress spoons made in a limited edition of 250 sets for the Fair. Each spoon, according to surviving records, is tipped by a dimensional bust of the actress and carries a facsimile of her autograph. While there is no surviving record as to who all of the actresses were, it is known that they included Sarah Bernhardt, Rosina Vokes, Mary Anderson, Annie Russell, and Fanny Davenport.

This event, in its entirety, marked the first time that "the theater" and those who worked in the theatrical profession were overwhelmingly accepted by society. Some of the event patrons were former President of the United States and Mrs.

≡ These commemorative spoons displayed the faces of the most famous actresses of the day. They were issued in limited edition, creating high demand at the fair. *The Actors Fund Archives.*

≡ The Actors Fund Fair was held May 2–7, 1892, in the recently opened Madison Square Garden. Using one of the most elaborate stage sets the New York public had ever seen, an entire "village," designed by Stanford White, was built on the floor of the Garden. The Fair raised $163,088 and was the first occasion in history when "the theater," and those who worked in the theatrical profession, received overwhelming acceptance from society. *Courtesy of Tamiment Library/ Robert F. Wagner Labor Archives, New York University.*

Grover Cleveland, Mr. and Mrs. John Jacob Astor, Andrew Carnegie, Augustus D. Juilliard, Darius Ogden Mills, J. Pierpont Morgan, William Steinway, Robert Stuyvesant, and Cornelius Vanderbilt. The 1892 Fair was a huge success socially but an extraordinary event financially. After expenses were paid, the Actors Fund made a profit of over $160,000. ⮑

Fifteen years later, a second fair was organized and held at the Metropolitan Opera House. Daniel Frohman arranged the opening of the 1907 Fair in a theatrical way. On Monday evening, the sixth of May, President Theodore Roosevelt pressed an electric button in his library in Washington, D.C., that signaled the start of the Fair in New York City.

When visitors to the Actors Fund Fair entered the opera house, they found it had been transformed into the main street of Stratford-on-Avon—where Shakespeare's home, Anne Hathaway's cottage, the

Copyrighted 1898 by F. Miller.

President and Mrs Cleveland

≡ Two of the patrons in attendance at the 1892 Fair were former President of the United States and Mrs. Grover Cleveland. Their presence garnered national attention for The Fund and proved to be politically beneficial when Grover Cleveland was reelected to office that year. *Courtesy of the Library of Congress Prints and Photographs Collection.*

≡ The official program cover for the 1892 Actors Fund Fair. *Courtesy of Tamiment Library/ Robert F. Wagner Labor Archives, New York University.*

SOUVENIR and OFFICIAL PROGRAMME OF THE ACTORS' FUND FAIR Madison Square Garden May 2.3.4.5.6.&7th 1892

"This event, in its entirety, marked the first time that 'the theatre' and those who worked in the theatrical profession were overwhelmingly accepted by society."

≡ A rendering of the inside of Madison Square Garden during the 1892 Actors Fund Fair. Images such as this one ran in newspapers across the country during the six-day event. *Courtesy of Tamiment Library/Robert F. Wagner Labor Archives, New York University.*

Guild Hall, and the Shakespeare church had been reproduced in detail. Hundreds of stage technicians had worked feverishly, at no charge, to build this English village in the halls of the opera house. Printers from as far away as Kansas City donated posters and fliers to advertise the Fair. More than one thousand musicians made up the twelve bands and orchestras—including Victor Herbert's orchestra—whose members provided concerts to entertain throngs of visitors, all for free. The Friars Club edited a newspaper for the Fair; the Lambs Club hosted an ancient inn; the Players Club brought a modern art gallery worth four thousand dollars, which included an autographed portrait sent by President Roosevelt; and the Twelfth Night Club collected souvenirs from famous performers.

Mark Twain and other popular playwrights of the period came to the Fair to autograph and sell their

≡ President Theodore Roosevelt opened the 1907 Actors Fund Fair by pressing an electric button in his Washington, D.C., library that signaled the start of the fair in New York City. *Courtesy of the Library of Congress Prints and Photographs Division.*

≡ Mark Twain greatly enjoyed his association with The Actors Fund Fairs. Standing in The Players' booth on May 8, 1907, he said, "I have had a delightful time—the whole afternoon. That is not because I'm just a human being but for higher reasons." *Courtesy of Photofest.*

works. In addition, Twain was asked to open the Fair, delivering this now famous speech:

As Mr. Frohman has said, charity reveals a multitude of virtues. This is true, and it is to be proved here before the week is over. Mr. Frohman has told you something of the object and something of the character of the work. He told me he would do this—and he has kept his word! I had expected to hear of it through the newspapers. I wouldn't trust anything between Frohman and the newspapers—except when it's a case of charity!

You should all remember that the actor has been your benefactor many and many a year. When you have been weary and downcast, he has lifted your heart out of gloom and given you a fresh impulse. You are all under obligation to him. This is your opportunity to be his benefactor—to help provide for him in his old age and when he suffers from infirmities.

At this fair no one is to be persecuted to buy. If you offer a twenty-dollar bill in payment for a purchase of $1, you will receive $19 in change. There is to be no robbery here. There is to be no creed here—no religion except charity. We want to raise $250,000—and that is a great task to attempt.

The President has set the fair in motion by pressing the button in Washington. Now your good wishes are to be transmuted into cash. By virtue of the authority in me vested, I declare the fair open. I call the ball game. Let the transmuting begin.

Although thousands of members of the theatrical profession donated time and talent, members of society attended in record numbers, and the Fair's popularity required it to be extended for two days, it did not reach the $250,000 goal. After expenses were paid, the Fair made $64,000 for the Fund—a huge amount despite the fact it did not come close to the monies raised at the 1892 event. ✍

≡ The 1907 Actors Fund Fair program. *Courtesy of Tamiment Library/Robert F. Wagner Labor Archives, New York University.*

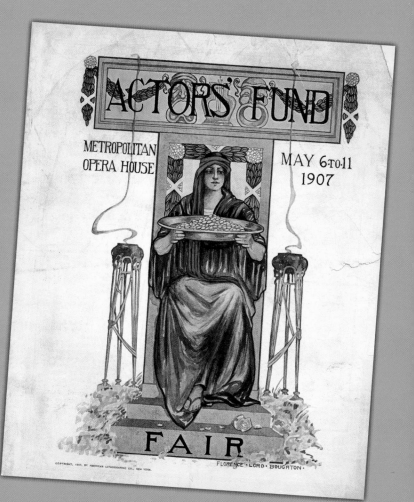

Having decided that the 1907 Fair was not as profitable as its predecessor because of lack of space, Daniel Frohman, then president of The Actors Fund, planned to have another Fair in 1910 in the cavernous Seventy-first Regiment Armory.

David Belasco, famed playwright, director, and theatrical producer, who supervised the transformation of the armory into the Gardens of Versailles, managed the 1910 Fair. The Fund scored a great coup—and attraction—for the Fair when President of the United States William Howard Taft agreed to travel from Washington for the express purpose of opening the Fair.

Special preparations were made for Taft's arrival. In the hall, white pergolas were draped with luxurious vines. Flowers were growing within a hedge of trees, and in the center of the hall was a court of honor, which was surmounted by Doric columns. As the President entered the hall, twelve girls bearing

≡ The Seventy-first Regiment Armory, located at Broadway and 35th Street, was the backdrop for David Belasco's replica of the Gardens of Versailles. The main floor was the garden area, with its elevated center hosting the illuminated Court of Honor. Within the Court, a pergola, measuring over a hundred feet in diameter, hung with thousands of flowers. *Courtesy of Tamiment Library/Robert F. Wagner Labor Archives, New York University*

≡ President William Howard Taft (1857–1930) agreed to travel from Washington for the express purpose of opening the 1910 Actors Fund Fair. Taft was presented with the Actors Fund medal commemorating the Fair. *Courtesy of the Library of Congress Prints and Photographs Division.*

armfuls strewed flowers in his path. Taft was greeted by a dozen of the United States' most prominent actresses, chosen by the country's top playwrights and critics of the period. The actresses presented President Taft with the Actors Fund medal commemorating the Fair.

A competition had been held for the design of this medal, and after due deliberations, a young sculptor named Chester Beach was chosen as the winner. Beach was thus commissioned by the American Numismatic Society to make the design. On the front of the medal, Beach placed three figures, with Charity protecting Comedy and Tragedy. On the reverse appeared the traditional theatrical masks. Taft's medal was gold. Reproductions of the medal were struck in silver and bronze and were available for sale at the Fair. This medal became the prototype for the prestigious Actors Fund Medal that the Fund has awarded since 1958 to deserving individuals.

≡ The 1910 Actors Fund Fair program. *Courtesy of Tamiment Library/ Robert F. Wagner Labor Archives, New York University.*

There were raffles, dramatic performances, and circus acts from Barnum & Bailey and the Hippodrome sprinkled into every day. "Buffalo Bill" Cody brought his Wild West show complete with cowboys, Indians, and a rifle tournament to the armory. Vaudeville magnate Martin Beck organized a playwriting contest for the best one-act play ever written that commanded a prize of $250 to the lucky winner. Many famous actresses had decorated elaborate dolls, among them

Lillian Russell, Marie Dressler, and Madame Luisa Tetrazzini, whose doll was not only beautiful but, by way of a concealed phonograph, could sing as sweetly as the great opera star herself.

The 1910 Actors Fund Fair ran from May 9 to 14 and came very close to realizing the profit of the first fair in 1892. When all the receipts were counted, the Fair had raised more than $125,000. ✑

True to form, The Fund was quick to recognize the needs of the theatrical community as new and exciting work began springing up on the West Coast. In 1916, the Motion Picture Campaign was created for The Actors Fund, and one of the most unusual events in The Fund's fundraising efforts was planned. To establish a presence in Hollywood and raise additional funds, a "Roman spectacle" production of *Julius Caesar* was produced at the Beachwood Natural Amphitheatre in Los Angeles. In a production reminiscent of the Actors Fund Fairs, on one hill the Temple of Jupiter was recreated and on the other, the encampment of Mark Antony's legion. In the foreground was a reproduction of an entire Roman street and Pompeii's theatre. There was literally a cast of thousands, including two Roman legions and hundreds of dancing

≡ This 1916 Actors Fund program was used during a benefit for the Motion Picture Campaign. *Courtesy of Tamiment Library/ Robert F. Wagner Labor Archives, New York University.*

Actors' Fund
=1916=
METROPOLITAN
OPERA HOUSE

THE GENIUS OF THE MOTION PICTURE WORLD.
"I'll put a girdle 'round the earth in forty minutes"—
SHAKESPEARE.

ALONZO · KIMBALL

≡ In 1916, the Motion Picture Campaign for The Actors Fund created a Roman spectacle production of *Julius Caesar* in Hollywood. *Courtesy of the Library of Congress Prints and Photographs Division.*

≡ A 1916 ad used in industry publications to raise awareness about the Motion Picture Campaign. *Courtesy of Tamiment Library/Robert F. Wagner Labor Archives, New York University.*

girls described as "gyrating madly" in leopard-skin robes. William Farnum, Tyrone Power, and Douglas Fairbanks played the leading roles.

More than forty thousand people attended the 1916 production of *Julius Caesar* to benefit The Actors Fund. Some traveled across the United States to see the spectacle for themselves, and it was reported that one man crossed the Pacific Ocean to do the same. The $15,000 raised for The Actors Fund would have been more, but counterfeiters printed 1,500 tickets and sold them for their own gain, a crime that was not discovered until after the event. ∾

THE HANDS THAT APPLAUD—

THE ACTORS' FUND OF AMERICA

SHOULD ALSO BE THE HANDS THAT CHEER.

McCUTCHEON

≡ Throughout the United States, materials such as this 1916 cartoon were used to bring attention to the plight of the actor and the need for an actors' fund. *Courtesy of Tamiment Library/Robert F. Wagner Labor Archives, New York University.*

the Friars and the Lambs clubs giving continuous performances.

Victor Herbert purportedly caused quite a stir when he entered the Palace carrying a pig, which had been donated to the Fund by the Florida Livestock Association. The United States Army, Navy, and Marine Corps had recruiting booths complete with the "most beautiful girls on Broadway" offering kisses in exchange for enlistments.

The climax of the 1917 Fair came when John Philip Sousa came out of a twenty-five-year retirement to conduct the United States Navy Band in an evening of patriotic marches. The Fair raised $80,000—an extraordinary amount of fundraising for any organization during these wartime years. ⤳

When the United States entered the First World War in April 1917, the Actors Fund Fair that year took on patriotic overtones. President Woodrow Wilson was unable to leave Washington to open the Fair, so he, like President Roosevelt before him, pressed a button that unfurled the flags of the United States and its Allies as Louise Homer sang "The Star-Spangled Banner" to a cheering throng of over ten thousand.

The Fair went from May 12 to 22 and was held at the Grand Central Palace. Though it had all the attractions and fanfare of past fairs, there were new and exciting additions, including a motion picture lot where visitors to the Fair could watch Mary Pickford, Douglas Fairbanks, and others filming. Harry Houdini and Will Rogers participated, with

≡ Though he could not leave Washington, D.C., to attend the Actors Fund Fair in 1917, President Woodrow Wilson took his cue from predecessor Theodore Roosevelt, pushing a button to symbolically "turn the lights on" at the Fair in New York. *Courtesy of the National Photo Company Collection, Library of Congress Prints and Photographs Division.*

Conrad Cantzen's Shoe Fund

One of the intriguing stories of Fund history began out of the generosity of Broadway performer Conrad Cantzen. A fine actor, Cantzen worked consistently throughout the early 1900s with supporting roles in several Broadway shows, but by the 1930s, his star, for all that it had been, had faded. He was living in a flophouse in the theater district, struggling for work. That he was poor could be deduced by his well-worn clothing, which betrayed years of service to the theater. Cantzen normally donned brown corduroy trousers and jacket. While the rest of him may not have been shiny and new, he was particular about his shoes. They were faultlessly polished, down to the hooks and laces. "It's an actor's business to see that he is always dressed in his best, and most important are shoes," said Cantzen. "They must always have a high polish and never be run down at the heels. An actor can't hold his head up if his heels are run down."

Upon Cantzen's death in the summer of 1945, a startling find was made when his Union City, New Jersey, hotel room was being cleaned out. He had amassed a savings account of $226,608.34, which he had specified in his will be used to set up a trust fund that would provide new shoes to struggling theater professionals. The will read, "…for the people who can't buy shoes, even if they are not paid-up members of Equity. Many times I have been on my uppers, and the thinner the soles of my shoes were, the less courage I had to face the managers in looking for a job." ✍

≡ The 1917 Fair program.
Courtesy of Tamiment Library/
Robert F. Wagner Labor Archives,
New York University.

≡ A 1917 Actors Fund Fair poster
used throughout New York City
to promote the ten-day event.
Courtesy of Tamiment Library/
Robert F. Wagner Labor Archives,
New York University.

June 8, 1882

The New York State Legislature officially passes the Act of Incorporation for The Actors Fund into law.

January 28, 1882

"*Professionals* [of the theatre] *are always ready to help other people—will they not for once, do something noble and generous for themselves?*" asked Harrison Grey Fiske in 1882. His conviction to create a safety net for the many professionals touring far from home and those unable to be buried in consecrated ground resulted in an editorial in the *New York Dramatic Mirror* entitled, "Who Will Start the Actors' Fund?"

March 2, 1882

At a meeting of theatrical managers at the Union Square Theatre in New York City, all pledge to give benefits for the fund.

July 15, 1882

First Annual Meeting of The Actors Fund.

1882

February 4, 1882

Actress Fanny Davenport, a reigning favorite of the day, throws her support behind the creation of a fund.

April 3, 1882

The theatrical managers of New York band together to make April 3 "Actors' Fund Day," with benefit performances to be held throughout New York.

March 13, 1882

The first Actors Fund benefit is held with the proceeds from this day's performance of *Sam'l of Posen: The Commercial Drummer* being donated to the creation of the fund.

1886

The Actors Fund purchases a cemetery plot in the Cemetery of the Evergreens in Brooklyn with twenty burial lots, ensuring that no one will be without a proper burial.

1882–1920 Logo

1910

The 1910 Actors Fund
Fair at the Seventy-first
Regiment Armory
is officiated over by
President William
Howard Taft.

1887

More than ten thousand
people attend the dedi-
cation of the monument
erected at the center of
the plot in the Cemetery
of the Evergreens.

1902

The first Actors Fund home for retired theatricals, on
Staten Island, is dedicated.

1900s 1910

1910

An established netw
"Physicians to the F
charge no fee to pro
referred by the Fund
ing impoverished ac
states across the co

1892

The first Actors Fund Fair is held at Madison Square Garden. In
attendance are President and Mrs. Grover Cleveland, Mr. & Mrs.
John Jacob Astor, Andrew Carnegie, J. Pierpont Morgan, and
Cornelius Vanderbilt.

1907

The 1907 Actors Fund Fair
is opened by President
Theodore Roosevelt.

1917

The 1917 Actors Fund Fair is opened by President Woodrow Wilson, who presses a button in Washington, D.C., that unfurls flags of the United States and its Allies. The display is accompanied by the "Star-Spangled Banner" sung by Louise Homer.

Al Jolson, star performer of the 1920s, donated his talent to Actors Fund Benefits throughout his career and continued this generous legacy after his death. Following in the tradition of The Fund's Planned Giving program, Jolson bequeathed a percentage of the royalties from his recordings to The Fund in perpetuity.

1920s

MOTION PICTURE CAMPAIGN FOR THE ACTORS' FUND OF AMERICA

SAMUEL GOLDFISH
CHAIRMAN

J. STUART BLACKTON
TREASURER

...rk of ...d," who ...ssionals ...are treat- ...rs in forty ...try.

1916

The Motion Picture Campaign is established in Hollywood with stars like Tyrone Power and Douglas Fairbanks participating in benefit performances.

A Brief History
of
The Actors Fund

1927

The new basic contract between Equity, theatre owners, and producers grants The Actors Fund the exclusive privilege of calling for an extra performance of any production playing on Broadway or the road, with all revenue from the performance going to The Fund. The Theatre Guild's production of *Porgy* was the first of what have come to be known as Actors Fund Special Performances.

1959

Construction begins on a new Actors Fund retirement home on the Englewood, New Jersey, site.

1961

Newly constructed Actors Fund home opens in Englewood, New Jersey.

1930s 1940s 1950s 1960s

1928

The Actors Fund Home moves from Staten Island to the former country estate of millionairess Hetty Green, in Englewood, New Jersey.

1955

The 1950s ushered in both "The Bread Basket" campaign and the Annual Blood Drive. A popular fundraiser, The Bread Basket collected money year-round from audience members at hundreds of New York and regional performances. The Blood Drive was held annually in Shubert Alley, combining the support of celebrities, producers, and theatre owners. Both campaigns successfully served the Fund through the 1980s.

1945

Actor Conrad Cantzen bequeaths his estate to The Actors Fund with the stipulation that it be used to help actors purchase shoes so they do not appear "down at the heels" when auditioning. The Conrad Cantzen Shoe Fund assists more than one thousand performers each year.

The Actors Fund, for everyone in entertainment.
Celebrating 125 years.

2007 Logo

2003

The Al Hirschfeld Free Health Clinic opens in New York. The Fund, in association with Columbia Medical School and New York Presbyterian Hospital, operates the clinic to provide free health care to the uninsured and underinsured.

2005

In the aftermath of Hurricane Katrina, The Fund immediately responded through its twenty-four-hour hotline for members of the performing arts community in New Orleans. Information and support were provided on location, with resources being distributed within twenty-four hours of requests for aid.

2002

Lillian Booth donates $2 million to The Actors Fund in New York to support the Fund's nursing home and assisted-living facility in Englewood, New Jersey. The Englewood residence is renamed The Lillian Booth Actors Home in her honor.

2000s

2008

2002

A star-studded cast assembled for the one-night-only performance of *Funny Girl* featuring sixteen different actresses portraying Fanny Brice. The sold-out show was part of the Fall Benefit Concert Series, an annual fundraising event that began in 2000 and continues today.

2008

In early 2008, The Fund will open Schermerhorn House, a 217-unit supportive housing development in downtown Brooklyn, providing affordable housing and on-site social service and health service programs.

2003

The Actors Fund's first program for "industry kids" is introduced in Los Angeles. Looking Ahead is established to assist young performers, ages twelve through eighteen, develop the values, skills, and confidence to make a successful transition into adulthood. Looking Ahead now extends services to performers as young as nine.

Gala Opening of The Shubert Theatre

FOLLIES
July 22, 1972
Opening Night Benefit
Actors' Fund of America

1980–1990 Logo
Brought back for 100th anniversary

1982

The Fund begins providing professional services, including mental health services, crisis intervention, and referral and advocacy for community resources and benefits.

1989

The Fund establishes the Chemical Dependency Program.

AN INVITATION FROM HENRY FONDA
LIFE MEMBER
ACTORS' FUND OF AMERICA
(Founded 1882)

Dear Theatre Friend:
Won't you please join me in adding your support to THE ACTORS' FUND by becoming a Life Member of this renowned theatrical charity.
Whether you are a member of the profession or one who finds enjoyment as a theatre patron, your help will be equally appreciated.

Thank you,

Henry Fonda
Western Region Committee
Actors' Fund of America

1985

The Fund creates the Career Transition for Dancers Program in conjunction with the performing arts unions. Now an independent organization, CTD continues to collaborate with The Fund to address the comprehensive needs of dancers.

1970s   1980s

1975

The Actors Fund Home adds The Percy Williams wing to the facility in Englewood.

1982

The Actors Fund opens the Midwestern Region office in Chicago.

1987

The Senior and Disabled Care Program is created to address the special needs of aging and disabled performers.

1988

A new nursing wing opens at The Home in Englewood as Philadelphia's Edwin Forrest Home merges with The Actors Fund Home.

1972

The Actors Fund opens its Western Region office in Los Angeles.

1982

The Actors Fund celebrates its one hundredth anniversary with the televised *Night of 100 Stars*, which featured hundreds of celebrated performers from every area of the industry. *Night of 100 Stars* was also produced in 1985 and 1990 as a fundraising event.

1990

This Benefit Performance of *A Christmas Carol* was directed by the legendary Zoe Caldwell and produced by Robert Whitehead. The Fund was further honored to have Broadway's newly restored Hudson Theatre choose this performance as its inaugural event.

PLAYBILL

HUDSON THEATRE

A Christmas Carol

by

Charles Dickens

1998

Through a partnership with the West Hollywood Community Housing Corporation, the Palm View Residence in Southern California, a forty-unit garden apartment complex for low income people with AIDS, is opened.

1996

The Phyllis Newman Women's Health Initiative (PNWHI) is established to help women coping with difficult diagnoses and the situations that result.

1998

The Actors Work Program, initially started in 1986 at Actors Equity, moves under The Actors Fund umbrella. The employment and training program has since grown to serve almost two thousand people annually.

1990s

If there were more people like you around we could all beat this damn disease!

You make me proud to be part of The Actors' Fund and the "Show Biz" community.

Thanks Ever So Much!

1988

After several years of caring for growing numbers of performers afflicted with HIV/AIDS, The Actors Fund formally established the AIDS Initiative with the support of Equity Fights AIDS. Providing comprehensive support and resources, the group joined forces with Broadway Cares in 1992 to create BC/EFA.

1998

The Fund, in conjunction with the National Endowment for the Arts, launches the Artists Health Insurance Resource Center (AHIRC). Through a national web database, seminars, and individual counseling, AHIRC provides the performing arts community with the most comprehensive health insurance resources in the country.

1996

The Actors Fund addresses the growing need for affordable housing by opening The Aurora, providing affordable housing and support services to working professionals, seniors and persons with AIDS.

For All Entertainment Professionals
The ACTORS' FUND
OF AMERICA

Late 1990s–2007 Logo

My Blue Suede Shoes, Courtesy of Mr. Cantzen

By Veanne Cox

> Perhaps the most unusual special fund which The Actors Fund has to administer is known as the Conrad Cantzen Shoe Fund. In accordance with the provisions in the will of a little-known actor named Conrad Cantzen, who died in 1945, some 750 pairs of new shoes are given annually to needy actors....He believed a producer would look to see if an actor were "down at the heels" and if he were, would offer a lesser salary than if the actor were well-shod.
>
> —From *A History of the Actors' Fund of America* by Louis M. Simon, 1972

≡ Veanne Cox, shown here in Times Square with her Conrad Cantzen Shoe Fund purchase, is a Tony-nominated actress with a career spanning Broadway, film, and television. *Jay Brady Photography Inc.*

After high school, and a few years at the Washington Ballet, I made a deal with my parents—instead of sending me to college, they agreed to pay my rent for my first year in New York City. I moved to the city in 1984 on my twenty-first birthday and was abruptly enrolled in the school of hard knocks; I acted in almost every rat-infested black box theater in the city. I must have pounded about a million miles of pavement. I survived those first few hellish years, but none of my cheap shoes did, including my favorite pair of white audition slippers. They were delicate but impractical. By the November of my second year in New York, I exposed their "holey" soles to my friend, Buzz Roddy, who took pity on me and offered me two great tips: don't wear white shoes after Labor Day and, secondly, The Actors Fund of America had a shoe fund for union members. You could get a $35 subsidy toward a pair of new shoes if you could prove you made less than a certain amount or were unemployed. There was a pair of shoes in the window of Otto Tootsi Plohound that I really coveted—a pair of blue suede shoes with a tread that seemed indestructible. They didn't have shoes like that in Virginia. I thought these blue suede shoes would bring me luck because they were both practical and theatrical—I guess because of the song. They had soles and soul.

The shoes were $55, marked down from $85, certainly the most expensive pair I'd ever bought—even $35 for shoes would be more than I ever paid. I brought my receipt to The Actors Fund timidly because I had never gotten anything for free before, and they reimbursed me. The shoes, after twenty-two years, have shown little sign of wear. They even received an ovation when I brought them out at the end of The Actors Fund performance of *The Dinner Party* in 2001.

They are arguably the best pair of shoes I have ever owned and the most appreciated. I can't honestly say I ever got a job because of my blue suede shoes. But they got rid of my cold feet, and they got me to my auditions and back warmly and safely.

The People

Actors Fund Presidents—
Past and Present

Brian Stokes Mitchell
2004–

Dubbed "The Last Leading Man" by the *New York Times*, Tony-winner Brian Stokes Mitchell has enjoyed a rich and varied career on Broadway, television, and film along with appearances in the great American concert halls. In addition to his many theatrical awards, he has enjoyed a long television and recording career. He brings a charismatic presence to The Fund in his latest role as president. His committed and untiring work has brought The Fund national attention, guiding the organization into the next 125 years.

Tom Dillon
1989–2004

Thomas Dillon was a true performer with a long and distinguished career in show business. In addition to his numerous Broadway, television, and film credits,

he and comedian Bert Wheeler were among America's most popular duos, performing on the Ed Sullivan Show and at the White House. Dillon's fifteen-year tenure made him one of the longest-serving presidents in The Actors Fund history, using his affable talents to steward the organization through a period of significant growth and accomplishment.

All photos courtesy of The Actors Fund Archives.

Nedda Harrigan Logan
1979–1989

Nedda Harrigan Logan, daughter of Fund founding member Edward Harrigan, began her career as a Broadway actress, later appearing in several films. Logan helped found the Stage Door Canteen in 1942 and later became instrumental in getting the first USO shows underway, starring in the first overseas productions. Logan became the first woman president of The Actors Fund—an organization close to her heart. Her passion and commitment made her an exceptional leader, with a particular talent for creating fundraising opportunities that benefitted The Fund during the healthcare challenges of the 1980s.

Louis A. Lotito
1969–1979

A native New Yorker, Louis Lotito spent his entire life in theater management. From his first job as an usher at the Hippodrome to his later years as director of the American Theatre Wing, Lotito was well respected for his generous spirit and keen business sense. Under his leadership at City Playhouses, hits like *Guys and Dolls, Death of a Salesman,* and *How to Succeed...* made it to Broadway. He served The Fund as a trustee, treasurer, and president.

Vinton Freedley
1959–1969

Vinton Freedley was a man of many talents but is best known as a theatrical producer and "star maker." His early career producing *Lady Be Good* began a lifelong friendship with the Gershwins. As a producer, he was behind hits like *Oh, Kay! Anything Goes* with Ethel Merman, and *Leave It to Me!* which introduced Mary Martin to the theater world. Before serving as president of The Fund, he was a faithful treasurer for eighteen years.

Walter Vincent
1941–1959

Although Walter Vincent's name is not generally known to the public, he was an important member of the theatrical community and a pioneer in the vaudeville and moving picture worlds. Vincent arrived in New York in 1889, playing small roles and working in vaudeville. It was there he began his lifelong friendship with George M. Cohan. A natural businessman and a genius for theatrical investments, Vincent enjoyed a successful and lucrative career. His greatest contribution to The Fund was his vision for the home in Englewood.

Daniel Frohman
1904–1940

Daniel Frohman's association with The Actors Fund outdistanced that of any other individual—spanning nearly sixty years. At the 1882 meeting to establish The Fund, Frohman was elected secretary, saying, "Everyone knew the secretary would have to do most of the work so I was unanimously elected." His work ethic was legendary, and as owner and manager of some of New York's most historic theaters (including The Lyceum), he is remembered as an instrumental figure in the organization of The Actors Fund.

Al Hayman
1901–1904

Al Hayman was known as the "father of the Theatrical Syndicate" and was acclaimed for his exceptional business ability. As president of The Fund, he continued the work of predecessor Louis Aldrich to bring the dream of building a home for retired actors to reality. His business background made him an excellent fundraiser, inspiring donations toward The Actors Fund Home in Staten Island and guiding The Fund into a new century.

Louis Aldrich
1897–1901

Louis Aldrich had a long history of leadership in the area of actors' organizations, dedicating his life to the concerns of the actors' wage and working conditions. A well-known actor, Aldrich worked throughout the country. His passion for an actor's welfare intensified after he was injured in a hotel fire while touring. He served on the board of trustees and was elected first vice president. His determination to establish a home for retired theatrical professionals paved the way for what today is known as The Lillian Booth Home.

Albert M. Palmer
1885–1897

Albert Palmer had more to do with establishing the direction of The Actors Fund than any of its founders. He had a minor claim to authority in the theatrical field, but his personality could dominate the likes of P. T. Barnum, Harrison Fiske, and Edwin Booth. A graduate of the Law School of New York University, Palmer eventually became manager of the Union Square Theatre. His business background made him a natural leader in The Fund's development, holding a series of benefits and securing a charter for the fledgling organization.

Henry C. Miner
1883–1885

Henry Miner began his career as an advance agent for vaudeville acts, including Buffalo Bill. This served him well as his career led him to theatrical management and the building and acquisition of theaters. Through the years, he expanded into retail and mining ventures. This extraordinary background benefited The Fund's financial affairs, and his natural leadership abilities made him a formidable president.

Lester Wallack
1882–1883

Lester Wallack came from one of the most brilliant theatrical dynasties of English origin. Working as an actor, producer, and playwright, he opened Wallack's Theatre in January 1882. Prior to his being officially elected as president of The Fund in July 1882, he had served as its provisional president from the time of its early organization. His contribution of resources was instrumental in the formation of The Actors Fund.

The Actors Fund Medal *of* Honor

First presented in 1910 to William Howard Taft, The Actors Fund Medal of Honor reemerged in the 1950s to celebrate individuals and organizations that enrich the entertainment community.

2008	Stewart F. Lane and Bonnie Comley
2007	John Breglio, Esq.
2006	Rocco Landesmann
2005	Roger Berlind
2004	Thomas C. Short
2003	Martin Richards
2002	James M. Nederlander
	Tom Dillon
	Related Companies L.P.
	Philip J. Smith
	Kevin Spacey
1999	Sir Cameron Mackintosh
	Bernadette Peters
1998	Gerald Schoenfeld
	Arthur Ochs Sulzberger Jr.
1996	Tina Brown
	Merle Debuskey
	Frederic Rosen
1995	Sir Andrew Lloyd Webber
	J.P. Morgan & Co., Inc.
1994	Frank A. Bennack Jr.
	Jonathan S. Linen
	Robert Whitehead
1992	Bernard B. Jacobs
1989	Lucille Lortel
1987	George Abbot
1985	Alexander H. Cohen
1983	George Burns
	Armina Marshall

1982	James M. Nederlander
1981	Ronald Reagan
1980	Nedda Harrigan Logan
1979	Frances McCarthy
1978	Bernard B. Jacobs
	Gerald Schoenfeld
1977	Mrs. Martin Beck
	Joseph Papp
1976	Louis A. Lotito
1975	Ellen Burstyn
	Charles Grodin
	Robert Preston
	Vincent Sardi
1974	Jacob I. Goodstein
	Debbie Reynolds
1973	Clive Barnes
	Harry Hershfield
1972	Alfred Lunt & Lynn Fontanne
	Harold Prince
	Neil Simon
1971	Danny Kaye
	Warren P. Munsell
	Richard Rodgers
1970	Brooks Atkinson
	Katharine Hepburn
	Ethel Merman
1969	Hon. John V. Lindsay
1968	Angela Lansbury
1967	Ed Sullivan
1966	Warren A. Schenck
1964	Angus Duncan
	Zero Mostel
	Floyd W. Stoker
1963	Lawrence Shubert Lawrence Jr.
	Newbold Morris
1962	American Shakespeare Festival
	League of Off-Broadway Theatres
1960	Nanette Fabray
	Sam Levene
	Music Fair Enterprises
1959	Ralph Bellamy
	Council of Stock Theatres
	Stephen P. Kennedy
	Mary Martin
	Musical Arena Theatre Association
1958	Actors' Equity Association
	Charles Dow Clark
	Fact-Finding Committee of the Entertainment Unions in New York
	Helen Hayes
	League of New York Theatres
	J. J. Shubert
	Walter Vincent

The Performances

From The Fund's earliest years, performances were one of the ways used to raise awareness and money for the organization supporting the theatrical community. On March 12, 1882, M. B. Curtis's performance in *Sam'l of Posen* was the forerunner of all Actors Fund benefits to come. At the influential March 12 meeting held at the Union Square Theatre, the date of April 3 was set as the day matinee performances throughout Brooklyn and New York City would be given to benefit this newly formed Fund. Some theaters and stars were so eager to move events along that they started giving benefit performances ahead of the designated date, with Curtis leading the charge. For the first time, notables of the stage mingled with the cream of New York society to raise money for an actors' charity. The benefit performance of *Sam'l of Posen* was the first in a tradition that endures today.

During the late nineteenth and early twentieth centuries, annual gala benefit performances were the primary sources of Fund income. These shows were more akin to special vaudeville bills or revues, segments of musicals, scenes from plays, and vaudeville headliner acts that were cobbled together by a skilled director from the attractions then playing in a particular road city and which relied heavily on the most popular stars then available.

Miss Civilization
By Laurence Maslon

"You're barbarians, and there's no place for you in a civilized community—except in jail." It's the kind of line that a high-minded society matron might

have delivered to a group of actors at the end of the nineteenth century. But, it was Miss Ethel Barrymore herself who delivered the line, in the middle of the star attraction of a 1906 Actors Fund benefit. No actress had captured the hearts of American theatergoers the way Ethel Barrymore had by 1906; her charm, both on stage and off, had captivated a nation.

For the January 26 benefit, producer Daniel Frohman—the brother of Ethel's frequent producer, Charles Frohman—had put together a terrific bill, so jam-packed with performers that it ran from one o'clock in the afternoon to 5:30. The benefit, staged at the Broadway Theatre, included the matinee idol William S. Hart, long before his cowboy pictures, as well as beloved actresses Elsie Janis, Fay Templeton, and Marie Dressler cavorting in various vaudeville turns. But the main event was Miss Barrymore, starring in the professional premiere of a one-act play, *Miss Civilization,* by her childhood friend and one-time admirer, Richard Harding Davis. Davis was the most celebrated war journalist and author of his day (he had covered the Spanish-American War for Hearst), but his one-act adaptation of a short story was an amusing, if slight, valentine for Ethel.

The title role was tailor-made for Ethel's talents. She played Alice Gardner, the heiress to a railroad fortune, who foils the burglary of her father's Hamptons estate in the middle of the night. Ethel, through a garrulous stream of prevarication, haughtiness, and seductiveness, manages to keep the three burglars in the mansion long enough for the police to arrive. It was a tour de force for her inimitable "civilized" charms. The three burglars were the mastermind, Hatch; a red-haired, jittery, Irish safecracker named

"Reddy the Kid"; and the elegant "Grand Stand" Harry Hayes—the handsome jewel thief. What made *Miss Civilization* a footnote to theatrical history was the up-and-coming young actor who played one of the burglars—John Barrymore.

John had joined his elder sister in a one-act play as part of a bill in 1904, while brother Lionel played in the other one-act. It was the first time—and the last—that all three Barrymores ("The Flying Barrymores—three, count 'em, three!" Ethel said at the time) would appear in the same theater (although not on stage at the same time). *Miss Civilization* gave Ethel her second chance to appear on stage with her beloved "Jack" (she only got two more opportunities—two brief one-acts in vaudeville and on tour). Although John Barrymore would go on to play elegant jewel thieves several times during his career, here—in the kind of conceit so beloved by benefit performers—he played the ill-mannered, trigger-happy safecracker "Reddy the Kid," whose face is so covered with soot that Ethel's character mistakes him for a black man.

≡ On March 12, 1882, M. B. Curtis, star of *Sam'l of Posen*, held the very first benefit performance for The Actors Fund. *Courtesy of the Theatrical Poster Collection, Library of Congress Prints and Photographs Division.*

The crowd at the Broadway Theatre ate up the one-act, giving Miss Ethel and her brother nine curtain calls. She had to ask the stage manager to douse the lights so the benefit could continue. The Actors Fund made $6,500 that afternoon, and it also made theatrical history because sitting in the orchestra, lapping it all up along with everyone else, was the third "flying" Barrymore, Lionel. The Royal Family of Broadway would make less than a handful of appearances together throughout their careers (and one of those was a movie), but The Actors Fund gave theater audiences one of those precious opportunities on a January afternoon, ever so slightly more than a century ago.

≡ Ethel Barrymore (1879–1959) was one of the most charismatic and influential actresses of the nineteenth century. She generously donated her talent to dozens of Actors Fund benefits, most notably in 1906 when she gave a rare performance with brother John in *Miss Civilization*. *Courtesy of Tamiment Library/Robert F. Wagner Labor Archives, New York University.*

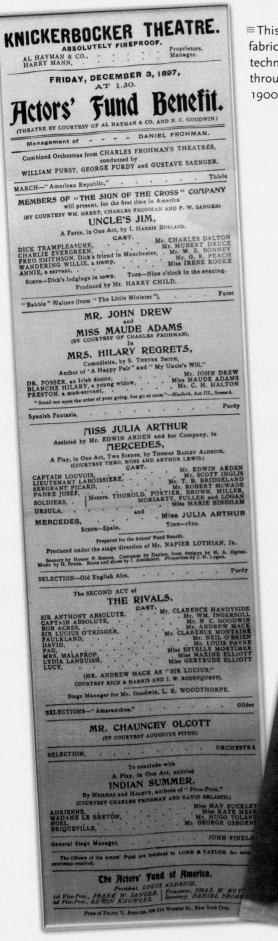

≡ This 1897 program, printed on silk fabric, showcases the advertising technique that was commonplace throughout the late 1800s and early 1900s. *The Actors Fund Archives.*

≡ Lionel Barrymore (1878–1954), the elder brother of Ethel and John Barrymore, began his acting career in Paris. Upon his return to Broadway, he garnered a reputation as an exceptional dramatic actor. In 1931, he won an Oscar for his role in *A Free Soul*. *Courtesy of Photofest.*

≡ John Barrymore (1882–1942) is generally regarded as the greatest actor of his generation. Along with legendary Broadway performances as Richard III and Hamlet, Barrymore starred in more than sixty films during his illustrious career. *Courtesy of Photofest.*

≡ During the early 1900s, The Actors Fund produced a series of annual events called "Monster Benefits." Each year, dozens of the top stars from Broadway, vaudeville, and opera would come together and perform specialty acts and scenes from various plays. These sold-out events were considered the hottest tickets in town and the souvenir programs (pictured), important collector's items. *Courtesy of Tamiment Library/Robert F. Wagner Labor Archives, New York University.*

≡ 1915 Actors Fund Annual Benefit program. *Courtesy of Tamiment Library/Robert F. Wagner Labor Archives, New York University.*

≡ Actors Fund program from 1915 benefit held in Boston, Massachusetts. *Courtesy of Tamiment Library/Robert F. Wagner Labor Archives, New York University.*

≡ 1917 Actors Fund program from an evening of benefits in Boston, Massachusetts. *Courtesy of Tamiment Library/Robert F. Wagner Labor Archives, New York University.*

≡ Vaudeville program from 1916 benefit performance in New York City. *Courtesy of Tamiment Library/Robert F. Wagner Labor Archives, New York University.*

≡ Stylized program from 1918 Actors Fund benefit performance. *Courtesy of Tamiment Library/ Robert F. Wagner Labor Archives, New York University.*

≡ 1921 Actors Fund Annual Benefit program. *Courtesy of Tamiment Library/Robert F. Wagner Labor Archives, New York University.*

≡ 1919 Actors Fund Annual Benefit program. *Courtesy of Tamiment Library/ Robert F. Wagner Labor Archives, New York University.*

≡ 1923 Actors Fund Annual Benefit program.
*Courtesy of Tamiment Library/Robert F. Wagner
Labor Archives, New York University.*

The years immediately preceding and following the stock market crash of October 1929 were critical to The Actors Fund. These were years marking profound changes in the entertainment world and in the country. The Fund's trustees saw the beginning of the first regularized source of income that the Fund could count on from within the profession, and they also learned to cope with the tough challenges of the Great Depression. As the Depression dragged on through the years 1930 to 1933, the ability of The Actors Fund to meet the demands made upon it was tested daily. In those years, prudent financial management enabled The Fund to meet its obligations fully and to satisfy the needs of financially distressed members of the theatrical profession. The Fund met its burden despite the sharp increase in the number of people qualifying for assistance and the rise of cost per case that occurred in the lean years of the Depression. The upward trend in the numbers of those in need and cost per case has continued through the years, requiring The Fund to increase its capital assets many times over to ensure sufficient funds.

≡ This 1931 design was the official program of The Actors Fund fiftieth anniversary gala. The Depression subdued festivities, with The Fund opting to raise awareness about the financially distressed members of the theatrical profession. *Courtesy of Tamiment Library/Robert F. Wagner Labor Archives, New York University.*

≡ This box office receipt from the New Amsterdam Theatre denotes the seating for a January 21, 1934, Actors Fund benefit performance. *Courtesy of Tamiment Library/Robert F. Wagner Labor Archives, New York University.*

≡ A ticket stub from a January 26, 1936, Actors Fund Annual Benefit at the 44th Street Theatre in New York City. *Courtesy of Tamiment Library/Robert F. Wagner Labor Archives, New York University.*

≡ An Actors Fund Benefit was held in Hollywood on July 1, 1936. *Courtesy of Tamiment Library/Robert F. Wagner Labor Archives, New York University.*

≡ This Actors Fund Benefit took on a patriotic flair when the Star Spangled Ball was held at the Hotel Astor on December 28, 1948. *Courtesy of Tamiment Library/Robert F. Wagner Labor Archives, New York University.*

≡ Times Square, center of New York's theatrical community, is pictured here in 1936. *Courtesy of Tamiment Library/Robert F. Wagner Labor Archives, New York University.*

≡ The 1936 souvenir program from the July 1, 1936, Hollywood benefit. *Courtesy of Tamiment Library/Robert F. Wagner Labor Archives, New York University.*

Actors' Fund
Benefit

Souvenir
1936

≡ This November 16, 1937, letter documents Lee Shubert's offer of the Imperial Theatre for a benefit performance. This support continues today through The Shubert Organization and Foundation, which consistently donates its theatres for special events and performances, and has contributed millions of dollars in grants to The Actors Fund. *Courtesy of Tamiment Library/Robert F. Wagner Labor Archives, New York University.*

CIrcle 6-9500

Select Theatres Corporation
236 West 44th Street
New York, N. Y.

November 16, 1937

My dear Mr Frohman

I will be glad to let you have the Imperial theatre Sunday night, January 23rd for the benefit for the Actors Fund.

Yours sincerely,

Mr Daniel Frohman
Lyceum Theatre

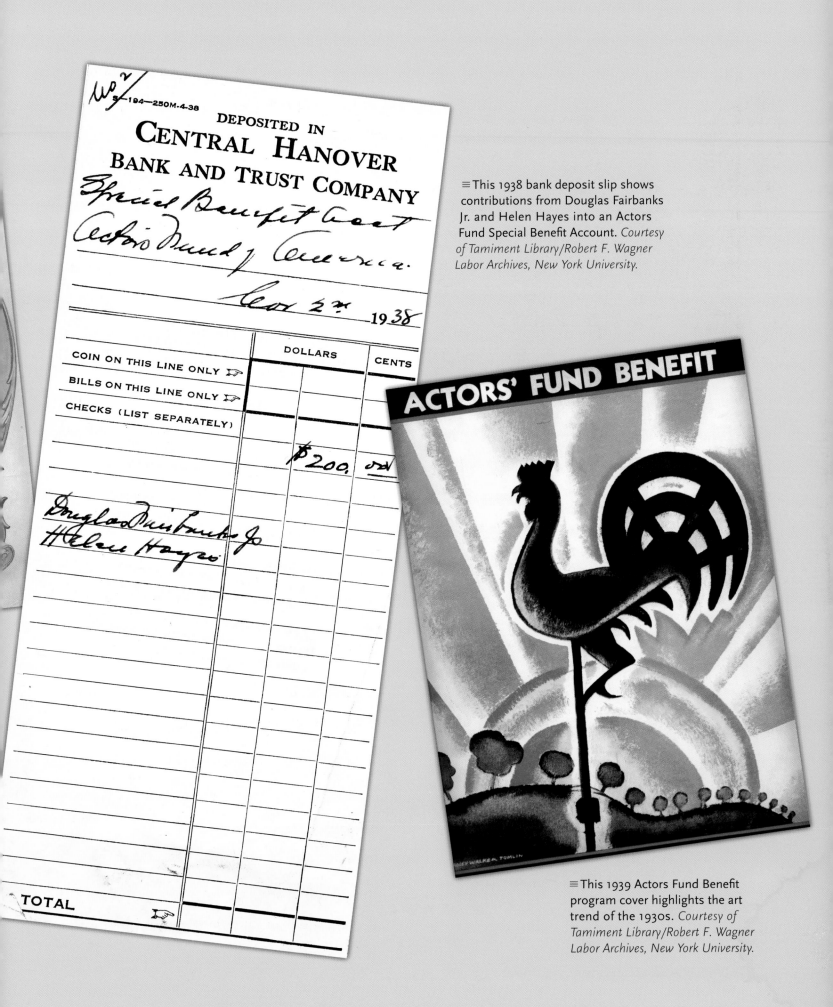

≡ This 1938 bank deposit slip shows contributions from Douglas Fairbanks Jr. and Helen Hayes into an Actors Fund Special Benefit Account. *Courtesy of Tamiment Library/Robert F. Wagner Labor Archives, New York University.*

≡ This 1939 Actors Fund Benefit program cover highlights the art trend of the 1930s. *Courtesy of Tamiment Library/Robert F. Wagner Labor Archives, New York University.*

I In 1927, an agreement was reached among The Actors Fund, Equity, and the Producing Managers Association that provided a giant step forward toward assuring The Fund a steady income from the voluntary services of those in the theatrical profession. This new basic contract with Equity, theater owners, and producers granted The Fund the exclusive privilege of calling for an extra performance of any production playing on Broadway or the road, with all revenue from the performance going to The Fund. The Theatre Guild's production of *Porgy* was the first of what have come to be known as Actors Fund Special Performances. This is an added performance to a show's regular weekly schedule—creating a nine-show week.

≡ The original show poster of *Porgy*, which debuted on Broadway on October 10, 1927, and ran for 367 performances. *The Actors Fund Archives.*

≡ *Carousel* ran from April 19, 1945, to May 24, 1947, at the Majestic Theatre. *The Actors Fund Archives.*

≡ *Kiss Me Kate* ran from December 30, 1948, to July 28, 1951, at the Century Theatre. *The Actors Fund Archives.*

≡ *Finian's Rainbow* ran from January 10, 1947, to October 2, 1948, at the 46th Street Theatre. *The Actors Fund Archives.*

≡ *The King and I* ran from March 29, 1951, to March 20, 1954, at the St. James Theatre. *The Actors Fund Archives.*

≡ *Peter Pan* ran from October 20, 1954, to February 26, 1955, at the Winter Garden Theatre. *The Actors Fund Archives.*

≡ *Guys & Dolls* ran from November 24, 1950, to November 28, 1953, at the 46th Street Theatre. *The Actors Fund Archives.*

≣ *West Side Story* ran from September 26, 1957, to February 28, 1959, at the Winter Garden Theatre. *The Actors Fund Archives.*

≣ *The Sound of Music* ran from November 16, 1959, to June 15, 1963, at the Lunt-Fontanne Theatre. *The Actors Fund Archives.*

≡ *Camelot* ran from December 3, 1960, to January 5, 1963, at the Majestic Theatre. *The Actors Fund Archives.*

≡ *Funny Girl* ran from March 26, 1964, to July 1, 1967, at the Winter Garden Theatre. *The Actors Fund Archives.*

≡ *Gypsy* ran from May 21, 1959, to March 25, 1961, at the Broadway Theatre. *The Actors Fund Archives.*

≡ *Pippin* ran from October 23, 1972, to June 12, 1977, at the Imperial Theatre. *The Actors Fund Archives.*

≡ *Hair* ran from April 29, 1968, to July 1, 1972, at the Biltmore Theater. *The Actors Fund Archives.*

≡ *The Gin Game* ran from October 6, 1977, to December 31, 1978, at the John Golden Theatre. *The Actors Fund Archives.*

As the Fund turned a century old in 1982, it was determined that due to the nature of The Actors Fund, a party for its own sake was not an appropriate way for a charitable organization to justify its one-hundred-year existence. Vincent B. Vitelli, then The Fund's comptroller, remarked that it was increasingly clear that The Fund needed a nursing or extended care facility to accommodate members of the theatrical community who could no longer care for themselves yet could not gain admittance to The Fund's retirement home because of their poor health. Vitelli charged one of their fellow trustees, Alexander H. Cohen, to determine how this money could be raised.

Cohen returned to The Fund trustees with an idea that he called the *Night of 100 Stars*. The show, held at Radio City Music Hall, was an extravaganza. Cohen had arranged not only a spectacular show and follow-on gala but also a red carpet to cover four blocks of Sixth Avenue from Radio City Music Hall to the Hilton Hotel where the ball was held. The event was aired by the ABC network in the United States and in more than 250 countries around the world. Two additional productions of *Night of 100 Stars* were produced in 1985 and 1990, bringing The Fund national attention.

≡ Producer and Actors Fund Trustee Alexander H. Cohen originated a fundraising event for The Fund's centennial he called the *Night of 100 Stars*. He arranged not only a spectacular show and gala but also a red carpet to cover four blocks of Sixth Avenue from Radio City Music Hall to the Hilton Hotel, where the gala was held. *The Actors Fund Archives.*

≡ The Radio City Rockettes and cast members perform the opening number at *Night of 100 Stars*. *Courtesy of Tamiment Library/Robert F. Wagner Labor Archives, New York University.*

PLAYBILL®

RADIO CITY MUSIC HALL

NIGHT OF 100 STARS 2

A Tribute to
THE ACTORS' FUND OF AMERICA
SUNDAY EVENING, FEBRUARY 17, 1985

George Tsui

≡ Radio City Music Hall is decked out for the first annual *Night of 100 Stars*. *Courtesy of Tamiment Library/Robert F. Wagner Labor Archives, New York University.*

≡ A Playbill from the 1985 *Night of 100 Stars*. *Courtesy of Tamiment Library/Robert F. Wagner Labor Archives, New York University.*

≡ Elizabeth Taylor and Grace Kelly are just two of the hundreds of stars who participated in the *Night of 100 Stars* production. *Courtesy of Tamiment Library/Robert F. Wagner Labor Archives, New York University.*

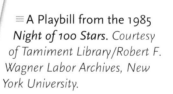

≡ The entire cast of the 1982 production of *Night of 100 Stars* takes the stage at Radio City Music Hall. *Courtesy of Tamiment Library/ Robert F. Wagner Labor Archives, New York University.*

S

Special Performances continue to honor The Fund and raise money to support programs and services. The top shows on Broadway, and the talent that brings them to life, repeatedly offer the generous gift of time and talent. In recent years, the cast of each Special Performance has autographed the official show poster. This extraordinary pictorial history of Broadway lives at The Fund's New York headquarters. Today, just as in the past, these performances are a proud part of The Actors Fund legacy.

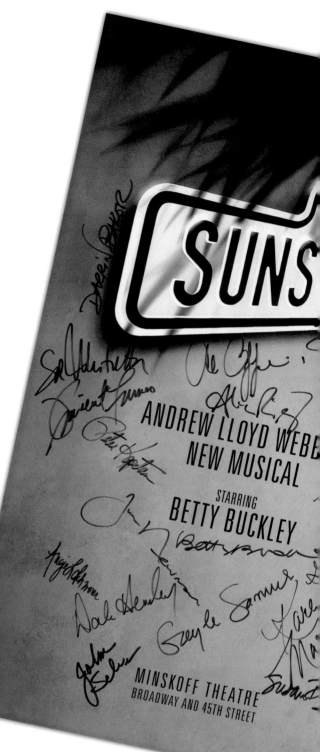

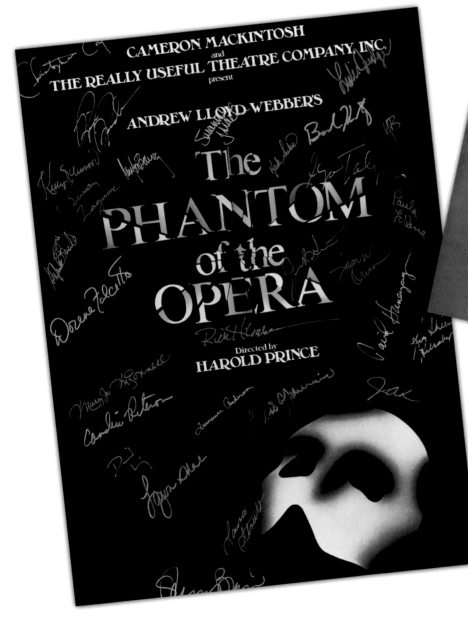

≡ *Phantom of the Opera* opened on Broadway on January 26, 1988, at the Majestic Theatre. *The Actors Fund Archives.*

≡ *Sunset Boulevard* ran from November 17, 1994, to March 22, 1997, at the Minskoff Theatre. *The Actors Fund Archives.*

≡ *The Producers* ran from April 19, 2001, to April 22, 2007, at the St. James Theatre. *The Actors Fund Archives.*

≡ *Lion King* opened on Broadway on November 13, 1997, at the New Amsterdam Theatre. *The Actors Fund Archives.*

≡ On March 28, 2004, the original cast of the Broadway musical *Wicked*, along with the company's musicians, management, and other personnel, donated their time and talent for the Special Performance. From left: Carole Shelley, Joel Grey, Kristin Chenoweth, and Idina Menzel. *Jay Brady Photography, Inc.*

SO MUCH HAPPENED BEFORE DORO

A NEW MUSICAL
WICKED
THE UNTOLD STORY OF THE WITCHES OF OZ

FORD CENTER FOR THE PERFORMING ARTS
ORIENTAL THEATRE
24 W. RANDOLPH, CHICAGO

**Kathleen Turner
Jason Biggs
Alicia Silverstone**

The
Graduate
A NEW COMEDY

Adapted & Directed by
Terry Johnson

John Reid and Sacha Brooks present Kathleen Turner Jason Biggs Alicia Silverstone in THE GRADUATE Adapted and Directed by Terry Johnson
Sets & Costumes Designed by Rob Howell • Lighting Designed by Hugh Vanstone • with Murphy Guyer Kate Skinner Victor Slezak
Larry Cahn Susan Cella John Hillner Jurian Hughes Judson Pearce Morgan Kelly Overton • Sound Design by
Christopher Cronin • Hair & Makeup Design by Naomi Donne • Songs by Paul Simon • Other Music & Songs by Barrington Pheloung & Original Artists
Casting Howard/Schecter/Meltzer • Production Supervisor Peter Lawrence • Technical Supervisor O'Donovan & Bradford • General Manager EGS
Company Manager Susan Sampliner • Press Representative Barlow•Hartman • Associate Producers Clear Channel Entertainment StudioCanal
Based on the novel by Charles Webb and the Motion Picture Screenplay by Calder Willingham & Buck Henry by Special Arrangement with StudioCanal

Tele-charge (212) 239-6200   ✆ Plymouth Theatre, 236 W. 45th St.   www.thegraduate.info

≡ *The Graduate* ran from April 4, 2002, to March 2, 2003, at the Plymouth Theatre. *The Actors Fund Archives.*

≡ *Wicked* opened on October 30, 2003, at the George Gershwin Theatre. *The Actors Fund Archives.*

≡ *700 Sundays* ran from December 5, 2004, to June 12, 2005, at the Broadhurst Theatre. *The Actors Fund Archives.*

BILLY CRYSTAL

Billy Crystal

700 Sundays

Janice Crystal Larry Magid and Face Productions present Billy Crystal in 700 SUNDAYS Written by Billy Crystal
with additional material by Alan Zweibel Scenic Design David F. Weiner Lighting Design David Lee Cuthbert Sound Design Steve Canyon Kennedy &
John Shivers Clothing Stylist David C. Woolard Projection Design Michael Clark Technical Supervisor Don Gilmore-DSG Entertainment Barlow•Hartman
Production Stage Manager Lurie Horns Pfeffer Company Manager Brig Berney General Manager Niko Companies, Ltd Press Representative
Directed by Des McAnuff Originally produced by the La Jolla Playhouse Des McAnuff, Artistic Director & Terrence Dwyer, Managing Director Presented in Association with Clear Channel Entertainment

🅰 **Broadhurst Theatre, 235 West 44th Street**

LIVE BROADWAY

≡ Billy Crystal and Brian Stokes Mitchell enjoy the after-party following the Special Performance of Crystal's one-man Broadway show, *700 Sundays. Jay Brady Photography, Inc.*

≡ *Spamalot* opened March 17, 2005, at the Shubert Theatre.
The Actors Fund Archives.

≡ Matthew Broderick and Nathan Lane after the 2005 Special Performance of *The Odd Couple*.
Jay Brady Photography, Inc.

≡ *The Odd Couple* ran from October 27, 2005, to June 4, 2006, at the Brooks Atkinson Theatre. *The Actors Fund Archives.*

≡ *The History Boys* ran from April 23, 2006, to October 1, 2006, at the Broadhurst Theatre. *The Actors Fund Archives.*

A NEW PLAY
BY ALAN BENNETT

The
HistoryBoys

DIRECTED BY
NICHOLAS HYTNER

NTNY
NTNY.org

BEST PLAY
2005 OLIVIER AWARD
2005 EVENING
STANDARD AWARD

Boyett Ostar Productions   Roger Berlind   Debra Black   Eric Falkenstein   Roy Furman   Jam Theatricals   Stephanie P. McClelland   Judith Resnick   Scott Rudin   Jon Avnet/Ralph Guild
Dede Harris/Mort Swinsky   Present The National Theatre of Great Britain's production of THE HISTORY BOYS A New Play By Alan Bennett   with   Samuel Anderson   Joseph Attenborough
Tom Attwood   Samuel Barnett   Bill Buell   Dominic Cooper   James Corden   Frances de la Tour   Rudi Dharmalingam   Sacha Dhawan   Richard Griffiths   Colin Haigh   Andrew Knott
LeRoy McClain   Pamela Merrick   Clive Merrison   Stephen Campbell Moore   Jamie Parker   Pippa Pearthree   Alex Tonetta   Russell Tovey   Jeffrey Withers   Designer Bob Crowley
Lighting Designer Mark Henderson   Music Richard Sisson   Video Director Ben Taylor   Sound Designer Colin Pink   Press Representative Boneau/Bryan Brown   Marketing HHC Marketing
General Management 101 Productions, Ltd.   Production Stage Manager Michael J. Passaro   Technical Supervisor David Benken   Directed by Nicholas Hytner
Telecharge.com 212-239-6200 • HistoryBoysOnBroadway.com ☺ Broadhurst Theatre, 235 W. 44th St.

LIVE
BROADWAY

≡ Lynn Redgrave shows off her tickets before the 2006 Special Performance of *The History Boys.* *Jay Brady Photography, Inc.*

The year 2001 began a new chapter for The Fund with Benefit Concert performances. These one-night-only events are produced by The Actors Fund and draw performers from all areas of the arts. From musicians to actors to pop stars and comedians, all-star casts are assembled and rehearsed.

≡ On September 24, 2001, at the Ford Center for the Performing Arts, a benefit concert of *Dreamgirls* celebrated the show's twentieth anniversary and inaugurated a series of annual one-night concert events. The cast featured Tony-winning stars Audra McDonald, Heather Headley, and Lillias White. *Jay Brady Photography, Inc.*

≡ *Tap Your Troubles Away* was presented on November 10, 2001, in Hollywood. This star-studded evening not only celebrated the music of the legendary Jerry Herman but also marked the first appearance of Angela Lansbury and Carol Channing together on stage. They each performed the other's signature numbers (written by Herman) with Lansbury singing "Hello Dolly" and Channing singing "Mame." From left: Carol Channing, Leslie Uggams, Jo Anne Worley, Angela Lansbury, Bernadette Peters, and Karen Morrow. *The Actors Fund Archives.*

≡ On September 23, 2002, an extraordinary cast assembled for the Benefit Concert of *Funny Girl* at the New Amsterdam Theatre. With Peter Gallagher as Nicky Arnstein, each song brought a new funny lady to the stage, including Jane Krakowski (pictured), Whoopi Goldberg, Sutton Foster, Judy Kuhn, Lillias White, Carolee Carmello, Bebe Neuwirth, Kristin Chenoweth, LaChanze, Ricki Lake, Idina Menzel, Julia Murney, Ana Gasteyer, Spencer Kayden, Andrea Martin, and Alice Playten. *Jay Brady Photography, Inc.*

≡ On March 30, 2003, Kirk Douglas and Calista Flockhart (pictured) joined Stockard Channing and Tim Curry in the one-night-only benefit performance of the Hollywood classic *All About Eve* at the famed Ahmanson Theatre in Los Angeles. *Jay Brady Photography, Inc.*

≡ Singer and songwriter Josh Groban in the Benefit Concert of *Chess* on September 22, 2003, at the New Amsterdam Theatre. *Jay Brady Photography, Inc.*

THE ACTORS' FUND OF AME
PROUDLY PRESENTS
THE THIRD ANNUAL BENEFIT C

Josh Groban Julia Murney Adam Pascal
Raúl Esparza Sutton Foster
Jonathan Dokuchitz Norm Lewis

Meredith Akins Yassmin Alers Albert Altovilla Kim Alvarez Carrie Ellen Austin Allane Baquerot De
Raissa Katona Bennett Stephen Bienskie John Bolton Jerad Bortz Kevin Bott Stacey Lynn Brass Rachel Bress Stuar
Lou I. Castro Lanene Charters Kate Coffman-Lloyd Katherine Lynne Condit Tim Cross Stephanie D'Abruzzo Justin Danie
Ryan Dietz John Treacy Egan Markeisha Ensley Mary Faber Phil Fabry Barrett Foa Robert H.Fowler Susan Fulginiti Laurie Ge
Tanesha Gary-Stickney Chris Ghelfi Brian M. Golub Sue Goodman Ann Harada Nina Hennessey Ra-Sean Holloway Stephen
MaryAnn Hu Cristin J. Hubbard Adam Hunter Jessica Jackson Natalie Joy Johnson Naomi Kakuk Laurie Kanya
Damian Keenan Trent Armand Kendall Michael Klimzak Gerti James David Ladd Anika Larsen Jason S. Little
David McKeown Naomi Naughton Darius Nichols Audrey Klinger Lynet Knapp Max Perlman David Petrolle Larry Raben
Charlie Schwartz Nicole Ruth Snelson Terri O'Neill Amanda Ryan Paige Shelley Thomas Ron Todorowski Grant Turner
Jessica Walker Nyjah Moore Westbmoks Lawrence Street Doug Storm Eileen Tepper Wysandria Woolsey Matt Zarley Kristine Zbornik
Jason Weston Schele Williams Gustavo Wons

MUSIC BY
BENNY ANDERSSON BJÖRN ULVAEUS

BASED ON AN IDEA BY
TIM RICE

LYRICS BY
TIM RICE

BROADWAY PRODUCTION PRESENTED BY
THE SHUBERT ORGANIZATION 3 KNIGHTS Ltd. ROBERT FOX Ltd.

DIRECTED BY
TREVOR NUNN

SCENIC DESIGNER
PAUL WEIMER

PRESENTED WITH SPECIAL PERMISSION BY
RICHARD NELSON
AUTHOR OF THE ORIGINAL BROADWAY PRODUCTION OF CHESS

PRODUCTION STAGE MANAGER
SHERRY COHEN

LIGHTING DESIGNER
JEFF CROITER

ALBERT
ALTOVILLA

MAKE-UP CONSULTANT
MAC COSMETICS

SOUND DESIGNER
CYNTHIA J. HAWKINS

EXECUTIVE PRODUCER
CATHERINE COOKE

PRESS REPRESENTATIVE
BARLOW • HARTMAN

COSTUME COORDINATOR
MICHAEL GROWLER

DIRECTED BY
PETER FLYNN

COORDINATING PRODUCER
ANDREW KATO

CONCERT ADAPTATION
TIM PINCKNEY

ADVERTISING AGENCY
SPOTCO

CHOREOGRAPHED BY
CHRISTOPHER GATTELLI

ARTISTIC PRODUCER/MUSICAL DIRECTOR
SETH RUDETSKY

MONDAY • SEPTEMBER 22, 2003 • 7:30 PM
THE NEW AMSTERDAM THEATRE • NEW YORK CITY
ALL PROCEEDS WILL BENEFIT THE ACTORS' FUND OF AMERICA • WWW.ACTORSFUND.ORG

SPONSORED BY
TONY DELLASALLA

The New York Times
TARGET
John's
HX MAGAZINE
KENNETH COLE New York
MAC VIVA GLAM

Ana Gasteyer brings her comedic flair to the Benefit Concert of *Hair* on September 20, 2004, at the New Amsterdam Theatre. The all-star cast recording garnered a 2004 Grammy nomination. *Jay Brady Photography, Inc.*

≡ Phyllis Newman and Lauren Bacall take their seats at the 2005 benefit performance of *On the 20th Century. Jay Brady Photography, Inc.*

CASABLANCA

THE ACTORS' FUND OF AMERICA PRESENTS

...because sooner or later, everybody comes to Rick's.

Original Screenplay By JULIUS J. EPSTEIN, PHILIP G. EPSTEIN AND HOWA

Screenplay courtesy of WARNER BROS. INC.

Screenplay adapted by
DAVID RAMBO

Starring (in alphabetical order)

IAN ABERCROMBIE · THORA BIR
DAN CASTELLANETA · BRUCE DAV
ANDRÉ DE SHIELDS · HENRY GI
SUZANNA GUZMÁN · ANNE H
EDWARD HERRMANN · KEN HO
ROB KAHN · TOM McGOW
JOHN RUBINSTEIN · CHRISTIA
HAL SPARKS · MICHAEL

with
ELDNE ALISON, ERIKA AMATO, CHRISTOP
TOM COSTELLO, STEVEN HACK, GREGORY HAL
HARRY MURPHY, ANNE O'DONNELL
ASHLEIGH SUMNER, MICHAEL GRANT TE

Scenic Design
JOHN IACOVELLI

Costume Design
MAGGIE MORGAN

Lighting Design
TOM RUZIKA

Sound Design
PHIL G. ALLEN

Production Stage Manager
MEREDITH GREENBURG

Musical Director
BRAD ELLIS

Event Chair
KATE EDELMAN JOHNSON

Casting Consultant
MARY JO SLATER

Publicist
B. HARLAN BO

Associate Producer
ROBERT SOKOL

Producer
SUSAN CLINES

Executive Producer
DAVID MICHAELS

OCTOBER 2, 2005
PANTAGES THEATRE

SPONSORED BY
GENE & ANN DICKEY
Continental Airlines   SMIRNOFF

GRAPHICS BY
DISIGN/STAMEDIA.NET

≡ On October 2, 2005, Christian Slater and Anne Heche took on legendary roles in the staged reading of the classic 1942 Hollywood screenplay *Casablanca*. The one-night-only benefit evoked the magic of a bygone era as the all-star cast performed on stage at the historic Pantages Theatre. *The Actors Fund Archives.*

THE ACTORS' FUND
OF AMERICA

PRESENTS

A WONDERFUL LIFE

A WONDERFUL LIFE

Book & Lyrics by SHELDON HARNICK
Music by JOE RAPOSO

Adapted from the
Frank Capra film
"It's A Wonderful Life"

Starring
BRIAN STOKES MITCHELL
JUDY KUHN
DAVID HYDE PIERCE
DOMINIC CHIANESE

...ael Berresse   Philip Bosco   Ronn Carroll   Chuck Cooper   Jayne Houdyshell
...g   Marc Kudisch   Phylicia Rashad   Marian Seldes   Karen Ziemba

... Anderson   Meredith Akins   Nili Bassman   Beth Blankenship   Harry Bouvy
...ietz   Barbara Folts   Jenifer Foote   Molly Gottlieb   Todd Alan Johnson   Cecily Kate
Marcy McGuigan   David McKeown   Bret Shuford   Matthew Shepard
...el Smith   Danny Vaccaro   John Wasiniak   Christopher Windom   Betsy Wolfe

Sound Design Bones Malone

Casting Mark Simon

Advertising Eliran Murphy Group – Jeff Matisoff

Make Up Make Up For Ever

Event Marketing Adam Jay

Press Representative Chuck Mirarchi – Apollo Public Relations

Musical Supervision by Jeffrey Saver

Production Stage Manager Lisa Iacucci

Production Supervisor Mahlon Kruse

Producers Tim Pinckney & Steven Yuhasz

Musical Direction by Lawrence Yurman

Choreography by Denis Jones

Directed by Carl Andress

ONE NIGHT ONLY!
Ⓢ Shubert Theatre 225 West 44th Street, New York City
All proceeds benefit The Actors' Fund of America

For additional information: www.actorsfund.org

MAKE UP FOR EVER   TONY DELLASALLA   the need to know The New York Times nytimes.com   John's   Casting in formation Subject to change.

≡ David Hyde Pierce brings down the house in the Actors Fund benefit performance of *A Wonderful Life* on December 12, 2005, at the Shubert Theatre. *Time* magazine called The Actors Fund benefit concert of *A Wonderful Life*, "one of the 10 theatrical highlights of 2005." The talented cast also included Brian Stokes Mitchell, Judy Kuhn, Dominic Chianese, and Karen Ziemba. *Jay Brady Photography, Inc.*

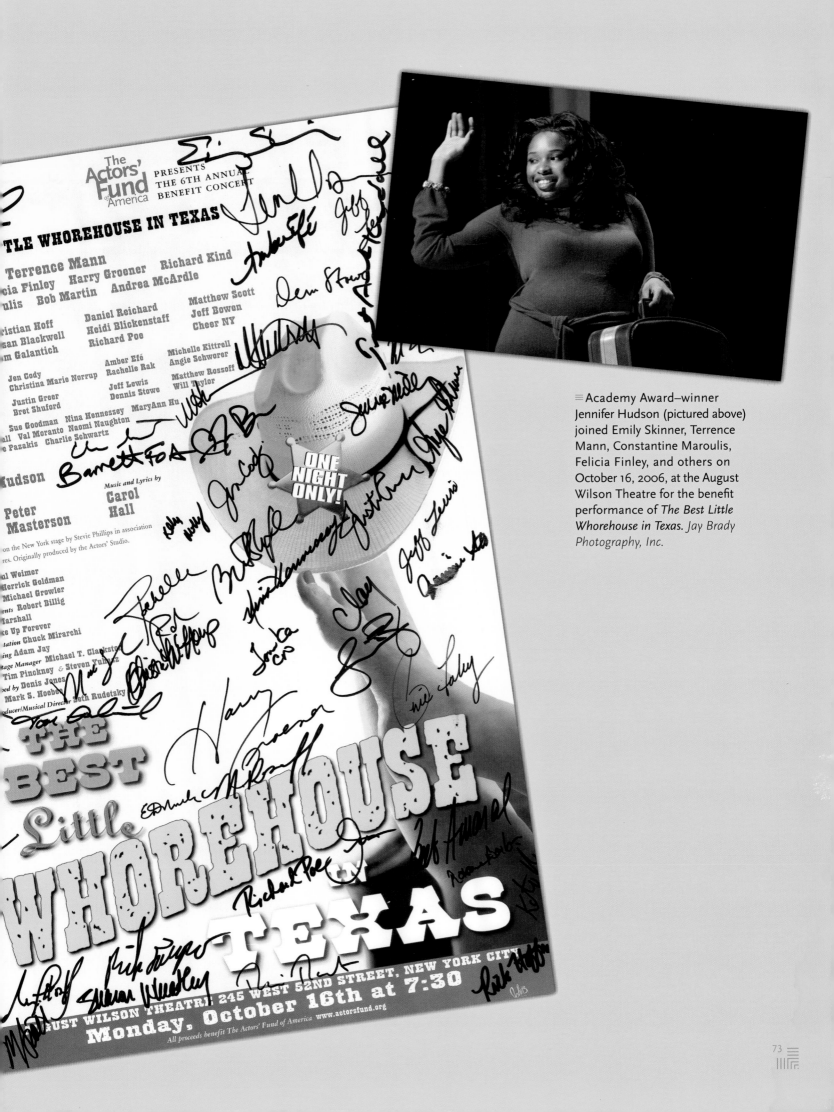

The Actors' Fund of America PRESENTS THE 6TH ANNUAL BENEFIT CONCERT

TLE WHOREHOUSE IN TEXAS

Terrence Mann   Richard Kind
cia Finley   Harry Groener
lis   Bob Martin   Andrea McArdle

ristian Hoff   Daniel Reichard   Matthew Scott
san Blackwell   Heidi Blickenstaff   Jeff Bowen
m Galantich   Richard Poe   Cheer NY

Jen Cody   Amber Efé   Michelle Kittrell
Christina Marie Norrup   Rachelle Rak   Angie Schworer
Justin Greer   Jeff Lewis   Matthew Rossoff
Bret Shuford   Dennis Stowe   Will Taylor
Sue Goodman   Nina Hennessey   MaryAnn Hu
all   Val Moranto   Naomi Naughton
e Pazakis   Charlie Schwartz

Kudson

Peter
Masterson

Music and Lyrics by
Carol
Hall

on the New York stage by Stevie Phillips in association
res. Originally produced by the Actors' Studio.

ul Weimer
Herrick Goldman
Michael Growler
ents Robert Billig
Marshall
ke Up Forever
ation Chuck Mirarchi
ing Adam Jay
Stage Manager Michael T. Clarkston
Tim Pinckney & Steven Yuhasz
ed by Denis Jones
Mark S. Hoebee
oducer/Musical Director Seth Rudetsky

ONE NIGHT ONLY!

THE BEST Little WHOREHOUSE IN TEXAS

EUST WILSON THEATRE; 245 WEST 52ND STREET, NEW YORK CITY
Monday, October 16th at 7:30
All proceeds benefit The Actors' Fund of America www.actorsfund.org

≡ Academy Award–winner Jennifer Hudson (pictured above) joined Emily Skinner, Terrence Mann, Constantine Maroulis, Felicia Finley, and others on October 16, 2006, at the August Wilson Theatre for the benefit performance of *The Best Little Whorehouse in Texas. Jay Brady Photography, Inc.*

Through the years, countless performing artists have presented solo concerts, productions, and readings to benefit The Actors Fund. Recent productions have included some of the top performers in entertainment.

≡ Reba McEntire, winner of fifteen American Music Awards, twelve Academy of Country Music awards, seven Country Music Association awards, and two Grammys, thrilled the crowd as she joined Brian Stokes Mitchell onstage at Carnegie Hall. *Courtesy of Shevett Photography, New York City.*

≡ Tony Award–winner Brian Stokes Mitchell brought the sold-out audience at Carnegie Hall to their feet. Special guest stars included Reba McEntire, Phylicia Rashad, Heather Headley, and Nikki Renee Daniels. *Courtesy of Shevett Photography, New York City.*

≡ Tony Award–winner Patti LuPone presented the 2007 Actors Fund Medal of Honor to John Breglio during the Brian Stokes Mitchell concert at Carnegie Hall. *Courtesy of Shevett Photography, New York City.*

≡ Tony Award–winner Christine Ebersole at a Benefit Concert held on September 26, 2006, in New York City. *Jay Brady Photography, Inc.*

≡ *Charles Busch and Julie Halston: Together on Broadway* was presented as a benefit for The Actors Fund. The wild night also featured Rebecca Luker, Brent Barrett, and Mario Cantone. Mr. Busch also held Fund benefits with the twentieth anniversary–staging of his show *Vampire Lesbians of Sodom* and a 2006 production of *Die Mommie Die!* in its New York stage premiere. *Jay Brady Photography, Inc.*

The Programs

You have given me great joy! I am proud to be a part of this profession to which we have all dedicated our lives. In some way, we all have made a difference, touching each other's lives both professionally and personally in many ways, large and small. There are none I love more than those in our business, onstage and off.

—*Colleen Dewhurst*

From the beginning, The Fund has endeavored to bring dignity to the performing arts community and acknowledge the unique challenges that come from a life in the arts. From the early years of proper burials, to recognizing the need of the aging theatrical population, The Fund has grown as needs have arisen. This philosophy has made The Actors Fund the national human services organization helping all entertainment professionals. All artists, both creative and technical, in theater, television, film, music, opera, and dance are eligible for the numerous programs and services developed by The Fund. With offices in New York, Los Angeles, and Chicago, The Fund annually serves more than 9,000 entertainment and performing arts professionals from across the country with direct guidance and approximately 600,000 more through Web resources. The Fund's programs are wide in scope and responsive in nature, and they produce significant results in the lives of those who enrich our national landscape with creativity, talent, and vision.

Homes

During the years 1885 to 1887, Albert M. Palmer was serving as the third president of The Actors Fund when one of the most ambitious undertakings was born. Louis Aldrich, a prominent actor and a vice president of The Fund, was a staunch advocate of a retirement home for those whose advanced age had reduced their chances of employment. Palmer's statesmanship in this matter led to his endorsement of Aldrich's project. It was necessary, said Palmer, on leaving his post as Fund president, "to found…an actors' home and hospital where the superannuated of our beneficiaries might find a pleasant retreat."

Aldrich, who succeeded Palmer as president, tried to convert the desire for a home into reality. After three years of nonproductive committee meetings, he turned to a fellow trustee of The Fund, Al Hayman, for help. Hayman promised Aldrich that he would personally contribute ten thousand dollars to such a home if The Fund could raise an additional fifty thousand. He also suggested that Aldrich approach the *New York Herald* for assistance in a widespread fundraising campaign. The newspaper entered the campaign with great enthusiasm, and in less than three weeks, the goal of fifty thousand dollars had been met and surpassed.

Within a year, in 1902, a handsome, Elizabethan-style mansion, surrounded by fourteen beautifully land-scaped acres, had been purchased on Staten Island, in a section called New Brighton. The Actors Fund's Staten Island home served its important purpose of caring for aged theatrical personages until 1928, when the city of New York decided to enlarge an adjacent park and took over the property.

The Fund thus acquired the former six-acre country estate of Hetty Green in Englewood, New Jersey. Green was the wealthiest woman in the United States in her lifetime. The mansion was demolished in 1959, and a modern, one-level structure was erected in its place in 1961. Fourteen years later, in 1975, the

≡ In 1902, an Elizabethan-style mansion, surrounded by fourteen beautifully landscaped acres, was purchased on Staten Island, in New Brighton. *Courtesy of the George Grantham Bain Collection, Library of Congress Prints and Photographs Collection.*

≡ On May 8, 1902, Joseph Jefferson (pictured here) officially opened The Actors Fund Home. *Courtesy of Tamiment Library/Robert F. Wagner Labor Archives, New York University.*

facility merged with the Percy Williams Home, which had been located on Long Island, and the Percy Williams Wing was constructed at the Fund's assisted-living care facility. The facilities were expanded in 1988 with the addition of a fifty-bed extended care nursing home, with the Edwin Forrest Wing being added after a merger with the Edwin Forrest Home of Philadelphia.

The Fund broke ground April 17, 2006, on the expansion of the Lillian Booth Actors' Home. Actors James Earl Jones, Fund President Brian Stokes Mitchell, and Executive Director Joseph Benincasa took part in the groundbreaking ceremony.

Today, the Lillian Booth Actors' Home, enhanced by continued expansions and provision of services, provides assisted living and skilled nursing care for all entertainment professionals, including designers, writers, sound technicians, musicians, dancers, administrators, directors, film editors, stagehands, and actors. Fascinating individuals from the world of stage and screen—actors, vaudevillians, Ziegfeld Follies dancers, comedians, bandleaders, and set designers—have resided here. Among the most famous residents were Joseph Sultzer and Charles Marks, better known as the comedy team of Smith and Dale, who were the inspiration for Neil Simon's hit play and movie *The Sunshine Boys*.

≡ The Actors Fund Home, pictured in 1928, was the former residence of Hetty Green, known during her life as "The Witch of Wall Street." Although miserly in life, her former residence provided a generous start to The Actors Fund Home and its importance to the performing arts community. *Courtesy of Tamiment Library/Robert F. Wagner Labor Archives, New York University.*

≡ An aerial shot of The Actors Fund home as it appeared in 1965. *The Actors Fund Archives.*

≡ This etched granite rock welcomes residents and visitors to the current Lillian Booth Home in Englewood, New Jersey. *The Actors Fund Archives.*

≡ Called "an earthmoving event," (left to right) Susan Lucci, Ben Vereen, Dorothy Loudon, Richard Kiley, Nedda Harrigan Logan, Jason Robards, Martin E. Segal, Ellen Burstyn, and Edward Herrmann dig at the groundbreaking for the extended care facility at The Actors Fund Home, later renamed the Lillian Booth Home, at Englewood, New Jersey, on October 23, 1984. *The Actors Fund Archives.*

"Today, the Lillian Booth Actors' Home, enhanced by continued expansions and provision of services, provides assisted living and skilled nursing care for all entertainment professionals, including designers, writers, sound technicians, musicians, dancers, administrators, directors, film editors, stagehands, and actors."

≡ Celeste Holm, Tony Randall, Ellen Burstyn, and Colleen Dewhurst cut the ribbon on the Edwin Forrest Wing in 1988 at the Lillian Booth Home. *The Actors Fund Archives.*

Social Services

The 1980s brought a great deal of change and expansion to the Fund. The Actors Fund began hiring professional social workers to enhance the financial assistance program by offering counseling, advocacy, and linkage to community resources. Services were designed to respond to specific, critical needs within the performing arts and entertainment community.

Erratic income, frequent periods of unemployment, lack of pensions, the need for "survival" jobs, and extended periods away from home are some of the problems that have a particularly strong impact on the personal lives of entertainment professionals. Because the work is sporadic, entertainment professionals frequently do not qualify for employment-based benefits such as health and disability insurance. All too frequently, performing artists "fall between the cracks," and when unexpected illness or trauma occurs, they have no resources to fall back on.

Senior and Disabled Services

The social services program expanded with staff focusing on the needs of seniors and the disabled. Helping people maintain their independence in their later years, the Senior Program provides connection to essential resources, financial planning, counseling, family education and support, and home and hospital visits to help coordinate care. The program also helps when people begin to need more extensive care and must consider options for longer-term accommodation.

Stepping in when people experience an unforeseen health crisis, the Disabled Services program helps people stabilize their situation and create plans to sustain themselves during recuperation. Whether coping with short- or long-term illness or disability, people can receive supportive counseling, financial assistance, coordination of care, education about benefits and resources, and advocacy services.

Mental Health and Chemical Dependency Services

The Actors Fund also recognized the importance of addressing the mental health and chemical dependency issues of those in entertainment and performing arts. Through its licensed clinicians, The Fund began providing crisis intervention, individual, couples, and group psychotherapy, and coordination of in- and outpatient treatment. With the increasing cost of treatment, The Fund negotiated reduced rates for treatment and offered financial aid when needed. Clinicians help address a range of issues including depression, anxiety, eating disorders, and post-traumatic stress. The Fund also helps those struggling with long-term psychiatric disabilities to manage chronic challenges like housing and treatment issues.

The Actors Fund Chemical Dependency Program was created to help entertainment industry professionals and their families receive treatment for substance abuse and addiction. The program has assisted hundreds of industry members achieve and sustain sobriety through comprehensive counseling and case management services. As with all Fund programs, confidentiality, respect, and preservation of dignity are hallmarks in the delivery of services. The Fund helps people recognize problems of abuse and addiction, and then develops individualized treatment plans. The Fund helps individuals obtain appropriate treatment regardless of their ability to pay. In addition, The Fund offers outreach and educational services to unions and employers.

Some Notes:

Please extend my thanks to the Executive Committee of the Actors' Fund of America for granting me a donation to pay my current rent in this emergency.

Also please convey my thanks to the Social Services group ... "the most untiring spirit in doing courtesies."

Please accept my thanks to you and The Actors' Fund of America for your generous grant.

I cannot express my gratitude enough for the support and grace the Fund has shown me.

I am profoundly grateful.

I want to Thank You for everything! The Operation left me pretty emotional and you listened to me and showed great care and concern. That alone makes me very greatful. I have always been proud to be a part of the Fund raising for the ACTORS FUND. Now I have a greater understanding of what an amazing source this is for our community. Thank you!

... my heartfelt thanks for the Fund's help in time of emergency. I am always astounded, gratified, and amazed by the graciousness extended by your office ... and I truly wish that I could've made much more of a contribution thru the years ... performing in four benefits (that I recall) and some weekly donations seems a pittance compared to the help I've received.

AIDS

When the AIDS crisis hit in the mid-1980s, The Fund quickly responded by creating the AIDS Initiative. These services included benefits advocacy, coordination of medical care and in-home supports, regular home and hospital visits, educational and support groups for the infected and their loved ones, a volunteer program, and extensive financial assistance for homelessness prevention, food, utilities, medical care, health insurance, and other basic necessities.

The HIV/AIDS Training and Employment Program was initiated to assist those with HIV/AIDS return to employment and/or engage in meaningful activity. AIDS Initiative clients are supported in developing action plans that lead to employment or to meaningful volunteer opportunities.

For twenty years, the HIV/AIDS Initiative has continued to respond as it did in the earliest days of the crisis, working with those who are newly diagnosed, those living and working with the virus, and those who are ill. The Fund's ability to take action has been a direct result of the creation and support of Broadway Cares/Equity Fights AIDS.

A Reflection by Tom Viola, Executive Director, Broadway Cares/Equity Fights AIDS

"But that day I woke up. Someone I loved had AIDS. How many more would there be? How long would other well-meaning people be able to remain as numb to this as I had been?"

Colleen Dewhurst wrote those words in her autobiography in a chapter about the 1983 Broadway revival of You Can't Take It With You. *In her recollection, she digresses from stories of rehearsals and life backstage with co-stars Jason Robards, George Rose, and Elizabeth Wilson to write of Orrin Reiley, then a young actor who played a small part and understudied the leading man.*

≡ Colleen Dewhurst at the celebrity table of the Broadway Flea Market, 1990. *Courtesy of BC/EFA Archives.*

Orrin Reiley was diagnosed with AIDS in early 1983 while playing You Can't Take It With You. *As so many did then, he kept his diagnosis a secret for as long as he could. But as pneumonia, an often quickly fatal opportunistic infection for those beset by this then unknown virus, weakened his health, with increasingly shallow breath, he shared his deepest fear with Colleen in the basement of the Plymouth Theatre before the rest of the cast had arrived for the matinee.*

Colleen did what she did best: she embraced Orrin—a courageous act in those early days of misunderstood infection—and insisted, as only she could, that no matter what turn his health took, he would remain with the show on salary so that he would not lose his health insurance. This was uncommon, nearly unheard of, support in a day when the afflicted were threatened with loss of job and apartment; when doctors and dentists would not treat them; and hospital orderlies would not deliver their meals. Fear of contagion was so intense, many were abandoned to die alone at home or in a quarantined hospital ward.

You Can't Take It With You *closed in January 1984.*
Orrin died in September. At his memorial service,
Colleen spoke to those in attendance whose calendars
were steadily filling with far too many such services,
mounting one after another:

"It is inconceivable to me…that nothing is being done
because this disease is about 'them'—gay men, people
of color, drug addicts and the poor. The venom of big-
otry, denial and misinformation we face is as deadly as
the virus itself. And Orrin, I apologize for my shoes. I
put on a mismatching pair today."

That day, Colleen's heart spoke extemporaneously to
what many people on Broadway, in all aspects of the
business, were feeling and particularly what those at
The Actors Fund were already too well aware of: that
we had been hit with a tidal wave of need for assistance,
crisis management, support, and understanding.
With nothing more basic than the grace and courage
to speak out without shame, blame, or benefit of syntax,
Colleen galvanized what until then had been much
hand-wringing into the beginnings of a coordinated
response from an entire industry—the theater community.

In 1987, inundated with quiet, desperate, and secret
requests for help, The Actors Fund created the AIDS
Initiative to address what had become its greatest
challenge to date.

Not long after, the Council of Actors' Equity created
the Equity Fights AIDS Committee, dedicated to rais-
ing money in any way it could to cover the expenses
of the AIDS Initiative. At about the same time, a
group of producers established a separate organiza-
tion, Broadway Cares, that would make grants to
organizations, including The Actors Fund, reaching
out to provide services for people with AIDS, their
partners, families, and friends.

If you were there, you know how terrible those days
were. If you were not, whatever you've heard or
might imagine, it was much, much worse.

It began small, as a true grassroots effort both on
Broadway and off, and in theaters across the country.
Bake sales, small cabaret performances, signed posters
and Playbills, and something practically unheard of:
audience appeals. Meanwhile, the first tentative,

≡ The opening number of the 16th Annual Gypsy of the Year Competition, just one of the events BC/EFA produces each year
to help raise much-needed financial support for The Actors Fund. *Courtesy of BC/EFA Archives.*

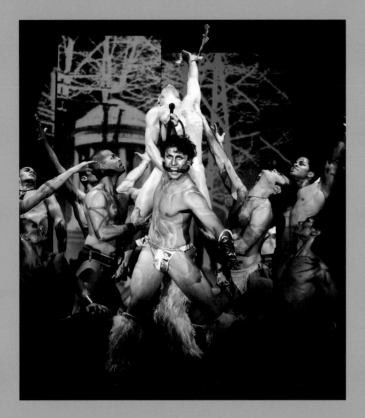

≡ Broadway Bares, 2007 continues as one of BC/EFA's most popular fundraising events. *Courtesy of BC/EFA Archives.*

scrappy editions were produced of what would become huge annual events; the Broadway Flea Market, the Gypsy of the Year Competition, the Easter Bonnet Competition, and Broadway Bares broke ground as the fundraising foundation for so much more.

Years passed and we grew with great emotion, occasional argument, and outbursts of measured success—the results of which, owing to a brilliant and unforeseen generosity of spirit, could be shared among us all, even as the client rolls at the AIDS Initiative swelled with those desperate for help.

In May of 1992, Equity Fights AIDS and Broadway Cares threw off their fundraising adolescence to join forces and emerge as a new not-for-profit. Broadway Cares/Equity Fights AIDS was born. One plus one equaled much more than two.

Again, it was not an easy process. We moved forward, now raising hundreds of thousands, and soon, millions of dollars for The Actors Fund's AIDS Initiative (as well as a national grants program, awarding

grants to hundreds of organizations across the country not affiliated with The Fund).

Cut to 1996 and the advent of effective drug treatments that allowed those infected with HIV/AIDS to step away from a definitive death sentence. However, that year was also marked by The Actors Fund's creation of the Phyllis Newman Women's Health Initiative.

It was simple. The ladies of the community who had so selflessly stepped up again and again for people— yes, primarily gay men—with AIDS would now see BC/EFA stand up for them. That year, BC/EFA made its first grant of $10,000 to PNWHI and promised ongoing support (providing over $4 million to date in 2008). Colleen would have had it no other way.

And so it has continued. From a grassroots fund-raising effort for people with AIDS, today BC/EFA proudly supports a number of major programs at The Actors Fund including the Phyllis Newman Women's Health Initiative; the Al Hirschfeld Free Health Clinic at The Aurora; the Actors' Work Program and the Dancers' Resource; two supportive housing residences, The Aurora in New York City and The Palm View in Los Angeles; as well as such projects as the New York Stage Managers "Unofficial" Health Directory, and more.

In short, thanks to the extraordinary generosity and support of the theater community since 1988 and through today, 2008, BC/EFA has provided more than $45 million to The Actors Fund, helping to maintain a safety net of social services for us all: men, women, and children in the entertainment industry across the country. (Another $48 million has been awarded to more than four hundred AIDS and family service organizations across the country.)

I was fortunate to have worked as Colleen Dewhurst's assistant from 1987 to 1991, during which time she was president of Actors' Equity, a trustee of The Actors Fund, and the chair of The Fund's Human Services Committee. Colleen's ability to remember *and sometimes even keep appointments—short of her dogged commitment to her work as an actress—was, at times, "lyrical." But she never missed a meeting of the Human Services Committee. If she was in town, she was there.*

Knowing how important the financial support would be to Actors Fund clients, as its president, Colleen insisted Actors' Equity make room for this rowdy, rule-breaking bunch, the Equity Fights AIDS Committee. She also insisted it play nice, indeed collaborate, with those folks from Broadway Cares. "You all must work together, bunny. Just do it. I know you can." And we did.

Before she died in August 1991, Colleen said over the phone from her sick bed at what would be her final Council meeting that June: "I am so proud of what we do for each other. There are many people who thought this thing would never go, that it couldn't be done. But it happened anyway because so many people came forward in many different ways and made it happen. And to this very day, I love you for that."

Since then, thousands have come together to make the work of Broadway Cares/Equity Fights AIDS possible for both The Actors Fund and hundreds of AIDS and family service organizations across the country. But they were drawn together by the heart of Colleen Dewhurst.

I have only one wish...that she is pleased. On good days (and even those that are "less than"), I like to think that she is.

So for now it all goes on—different, expanded, abbreviated, with great support, occasional criticism and, for me, always, a profound sense of wonder.

But, all of this sprung more than twenty years ago from Colleen's unequivocal, simple promise to a very frightened young man:

"Orrin, no matter what is wrong, I love you."

Phyllis Newman
Women's Health Initiative

Phyllis Newman

I understand the unique challenges women face in all areas of the industry. But, what I did not know, until my own battle with breast cancer, was how those challenges intensified when an unexpected diagnosis takes center stage. My experience propelled me to reach out and become an advocate and activist for the needs of all women, but most particularly those in the entertainment and performing arts community.

In 1996, The Actors Fund created a special program to provide a safety net for women in the entertainment industry who are coping with critical health concerns. They named it for me, and I am so proud to be leading this unique and essential program. We address the myriad of concerns women face when dealing with a serious medical condition. When women come to The Fund after a serious medical

≡ Trustee Phyllis Newman spearheads her Women's Health Initiative with The Actors Fund. *The Actors Fund Archives.*

≡ The Phyllis Newman Women's Health Initiative receives significant annual support from the Entertainment Industry Foundation as one of a handful of beneficiaries of the annual Revlon Walk/Run. The Actors Fund New York and Los Angeles teams are led by Fund Vice President Lynn Redgrave, shown here (center) with supporters. As of 2008, more than $775,000 has been donated by EIF to The Fund because of the Revlon Walk/Run. *Jay Brady Photography, Inc.*

diagnosis, they are often overwhelmed with concerns about their ability to work, family issues, managing basic bills as well as medical bills, and coping both physically and mentally with a challenging medical situation.

The comprehensive nature of our case management approach encompasses employment, economic, and other factors that impact each client's ability to fight for her health with maximum success. Case workers are effective at helping women deal with difficulties triggered by medical conditions and the subsequent challenges around financial, psychological, and family issues, staying involved with clients on an ongoing basis, and providing the support and referrals they need to best cope with these pressing issues. Counselors offer vital assistance in treatment and recovery, applying for benefits, filing insurance claims, coordinating childcare, and devising financial plans.

Support groups offered by the Phyllis Newman Women's Health Initiative (PNWHI) provide a place where women can come together to offer and receive support around issues ranging from managing chronic physical and mental health conditions to aging in the industry, and anti-violence and family issues. The Women's HIV Outreach and Education Program offers comprehensive services for women in the entertainment industry concerned about safer sex, HIV, or other sexually transmitted diseases. In addition, the Women's Health Initiative provides an extensive resource library and access to a vast network of women's health care providers, research studies, and other resources.

The goal of PNWHI has always been to support, guide, and empower women to navigate the unknown waters of a serious diagnosis. Together with The Fund, we continue this essential work. ❧

"Each year, we present Nothing Like a Dame *and bring together the brightest female talent to highlight our services and remind women that they are not alone."*

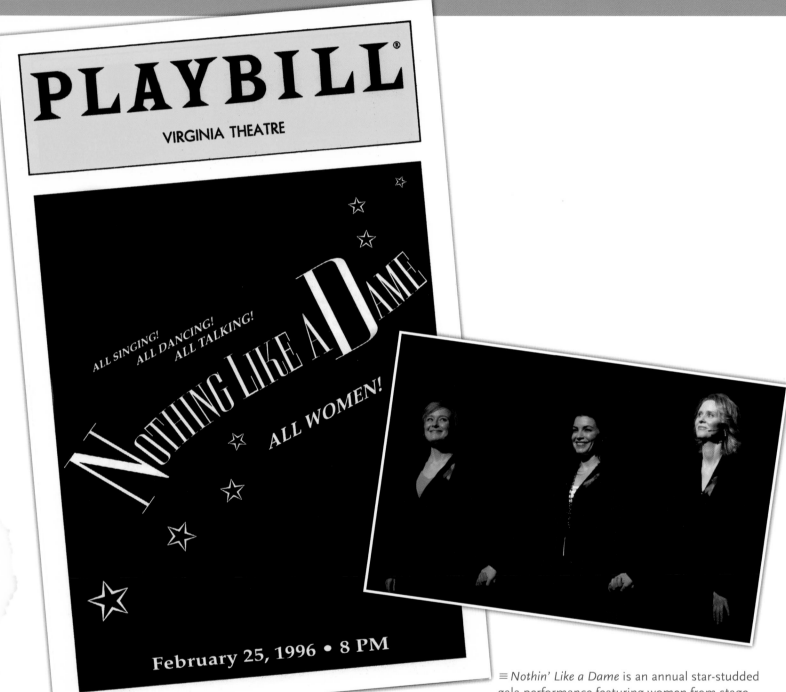

PLAYBILL®

VIRGINIA THEATRE

ALL SINGING! ALL DANCING! ALL TALKING!

NOTHING LIKE A DAME

ALL WOMEN!

February 25, 1996 • 8 PM

≡ *Nothin' Like a Dame* is an annual star-studded gala performance featuring women from stage, film, and the performing arts. Above, Jennifer Ehle, Julianna Margulies, and Cynthia Nixon perform at this one-night-only event to support the Phyllis Newman Women's Health Initiative. *Courtesy of Ken Blauvelt/Studio 66.*

Health Services

Health Insurance Resources

HIRC

With seed funding from the National Endowment for the Arts, The Actors Fund launched the Artists Health Insurance Resource Center (AHIRC) in 1998 to provide information for obtaining health insurance or affordable health care for the uninsured. Through a national web-based database, seminars, and individual counseling, HIRC provides the most comprehensive health insurance resource program for the arts nationwide.

Information provided on a state by state basis includes all available self-pay insurance plans, association plans, union and guild plans, government-subsidized plans, Medicaid, Medicare, artist resources and disease-specific organizations. The program provides information and resources to solve insurance-related problems and access medical care. The program works to foster the creation of more insurance options for its constituents by representing them to providers, highlighting the need for resources and action by acting as a spokesperson for the industry's uninsured, and advocating for change in legislation and government programs.

COBRA Continuation

Jerry Stiller

When the New York legislature passed, in August 2004, an unprecedented bill that offered health insurance premium payment assistance to entertainment industry members, it was the culmination of an intense four-year grassroots effort organized and led by The Actors Fund.

Known as the New York State Insurance Continuation Assistance Program, the bill sets aside $3 million in funds annually to pay half the COBRA premiums,

currently well over $400 for an individual and three times that for a family, for income-eligible union members who have lost their health benefits.

This meets a critical need, because in any twelve-month period, more than a third of those receiving health insurance from entertainment industry union health funds lose their eligibility, and most of those who are offered continuation are simply unable to afford it.

To achieve this success, industry unions, guilds, social service agencies, producers, and theater owners formed a coalition, with the four largest performers unions—Equity, SAG, AFTRA, and AF of M Local 802—providing the funds needed to organize and to hire a lobbyist. Meeting once a month, they developed strategies and talking points to keep the bill alive through the vicissitudes of political action.

The vibrant grassroots campaign involved bus trips to Albany where union members presented their case, bolstered by the importance of the entertainment industry to New York State's economy, to legislators and their

≡ Jerry Stiller, longtime supporter of The Fund, worked tirelessley to make the New York State Insurance Continuation Assistance Program a reality. *Courtesy of Tony Esparza/CBS.*

staffs, voluminous postcard and e-mailings to persuade undecided lawmakers, and a petition sent to the governor's office signed by the cast and crew of every Broadway show on the boards during the summer of 2003.

Many well-known performers participated in the effort. For my part, I lobbied Sheldon Silver, Speaker of the Assembly, who would twice bring the bill to a successful vote. It's all moot as to whether my going into a Seinfeld rant at a legislative hearing in Albany, my support of the Speaker on neighborhood issues, or a breakfast at a union gathering can be called "lobbying," but we two Lower East Side kids really enjoyed sharing stories about the closely aligned fields of politics and show business. The New York State Senate and the Assembly did finally see the wisdom in passing this bill and the governor in signing it.

At this writing, almost 1,500 entertainment industry members and their families have benefited from the passage of this bill, most of whom would have been uninsured for all or part of the time they were ineligible for a union plan.

Throughout the struggle for the COBRA subsidy, The Actors Fund unfailingly energized and inspired the participants, never letting any of us forget our ultimate goal: to assist the members of our profession in their time of need.

But that is what The Actors Fund has been doing for 125 years.

The Actors Work Program

In the mid-1980s, Joan Lowell, a stage actress and Actors' Equity council member, founded the Actors Work Program. With the support of the Actors' Equity Association and other performing arts unions, the program was initiated to help members of the theatrical community identify and obtain rewarding, complementary outside work. In 1998, this program moved completely under the umbrella of The Actors Fund, now providing group and individual career counseling, job training and tuition assistance, and job placement to more than two thousand participants annually.

The Actors Work Program is the nation's only workforce development program tailor-made solely to the needs of the entire performing arts entertainment community. Because of the episodic and competitive nature of the performing arts entertainment industry, there is often a need for additional employment in other industries. The Actors Work Program helps clients identify and obtain work outside their craft that is rewarding and complements the individual's primary career. The program works with employers in both New York and Los Angeles in creating job opportunities.

Thank you for your time and understanding in engineering all the assistance I've received. The bills are paid and my dignity is intact.
I am one lucky broad!
Here's to love, luck and laughter!

I would like to take this opportunity to thank you all for your assistance in helping me to put my life back together. I am very greatful for your assistance & doubt seriously wether I could have made this "spiritual comeback" without you.

A sincere and heartfelt note of thanks "to you and the Actors' Fund for your generous grant in paying for my Health Insurance Premium for March '06. The Actors' Fund has been a source of Assistance & Strength for which I will be forever grateful.

If there were more people like you around we could all beat this damn disease!

You make me proud to be part of The Actors' Fund and the "Show Biz" commun...

Thanks Ever So Much.

As you know, Billy died July 17th after a long battle with AIDS. Our experience was aided so much by the compassion you showed us as well as your eagerness to do anything & everything you could to help. You have the rare ability to put people at ease, we felt as though we knew you.

Please accept my heartfelt thanks for your support over the last 15 months. Your work will never be unappreciated.

Sorry it's taken me so long to tell you how much I appreciate having had the Money Awareness Program experience -- but of course it's not over yet since we're going to have a follow-up early in December.

But the program was, and continues to be, of great help in several ways; and I think this was the consensus-feeling of my group-mates, too.

I sure admire the creative thinking that comes up with these ways of helping actors help themselves, and I'm sure such efforts will strengthen the Fund in the future.

The Dancers' Resource

Bebe Neuwirth

Words don't seem to be able to express adequately the experience of seeing dancers with all the breathtaking grace, meticulous skill, and the raw talent necessary to excel in this field. Dance has been a part of our creative expression since the beginning of time, and dance is difficult to describe. Its poetry, lyricism, and romance reach across all cultures and have the ability to transport, elevate, and inspire our thinking. Dancers are a class unto themselves. They are motivated by the need to do what they love and are as dedicated as the most celebrated athlete. Dancers must dance.

Those who dedicate their lives to dance are confronted with a breathtaking array of challenges. The heartbreak of dance is that it is an incredibly difficult way to earn a living. Aside from the competition for a place in a show or company, dancers also deal with the constant threat of injury and the natural aging of the body. When their instrument of expression no longer functions, dancers are assaulted physically and psychologically with the impending end of their livelihood. The profession offers limited employment opportunities, low or non-paying jobs, and often a lack of dependable health care coverage. Dancers are constantly challenged economically and physically, maybe more than others in the entertainment professions.

For several years, I suffered intense physical pain that eventually led to hip replacement surgery. It came after several years of physical therapy, arthroscopic surgery, and excruciating pain. Following the surgery, I struggled with the emotional distress and possible ramifications of my surgery. Add to that the emotional stress of not being able to dance and not wanting people to know about my condition—and I think you understand what that prison is like. After the replacement, I recognized how extremely lucky I was to have a great doctor and great support from the few people with whom I shared my secret. And so, I wanted to create a similar

support system and presented to The Fund the need to address all the unique challenges and difficult situations that dancers face daily.

The Dancers' Resource offers a wide range of vital programs to address specific needs—including seminars and groups for dancers dealing with injuries or other health concerns—while serving as a

≡ Neuwirth, an accomplished Broadway dancer, a two-time Emmy award–winning actress, and a two-time Tony award winner, is also The Fund's third vice president. *Photo by Howard Schatz.*

The Al Hirschfeld Free Health Clinic

Founded in 2003, the Al Hirschfeld Free Health Clinic plays a unique role as medical provider for the performing arts' uninsured in the metropolitan New York City area. In association with Columbia Medical School and New York Presbyterian Hospital, the Hirschfeld Clinic ensures that no performing artist delays care or goes untreated because of lack of insurance or an inability to pay. Named for the greatest theatrical caricaturist, the clinic provides free health care and referral services and offers primary and specialty care, health screenings, and wellness education. Supporting a full-time medical director are many wonderful physicians who volunteer in the clinic or provide care to our patients in their own offices, free of charge. All of the clinic's lab work is generously donated by Bio-Reference Labs.

≡ In 2008, the Professional Dancers Society celebrated ten years of partnership with The Actors Fund, donating more than $1.2 million to help dancers in need. This partnership will continue to strengthen through The Dancers' Resource. On hand at a recent fundraising event were Chita Rivera, Joe Tremaine, PDS chair Joni Berry, and current PDS president Mitzi Gaynor. *The Actors Fund Archives.*

support system so that dancers don't have to face critical situations on their own. With assistance from Broadway Cares/Equity Fights AIDS, The Actors Fund has hired a full-time social worker for The Dancers' Resource. The Resource will soon have a web component on The Actors Fund site that creates an online community and links dancers to additional resources, giving dancers a place they can go to safely and confidentially address their unique and complicated challenges.

My hope is that The Dancers' Resource will help us all keep dancing, stay healthy, and enjoy our beautiful gift as long as we can.

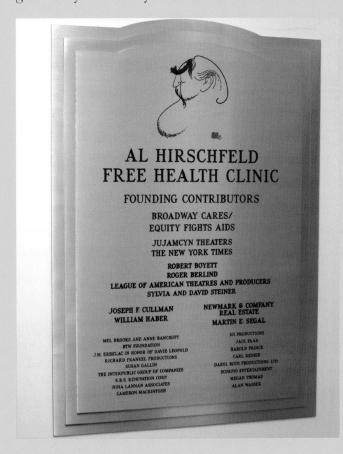

≡ The generosity and support of those committed to providing free health care to the uninsured and underinsured is memorialized at the Hirschfeld Clinic's entrance. *Jay Brady Photography, Inc.*

Youth Services

Looking Ahead

Looking Ahead, The Actors Fund's program for "industry kids" was introduced in Los Angeles in 2003. Inspired by the SAG/AFTRA Young Performers Committee and supported through the Screen Actors Guild-Producers Industry Advancement & Cooperative Fund and the American Federation of Television and Radio Artists-Industry Cooperative Fund, Looking Ahead was established to assist young performers develop the necessary values, skills, and confidence to make a successful transition to adulthood. The Looking Ahead program helps young actors, ages nine through eighteen, and their families address the unique issues associated with working in the entertainment industry. The program has created a community where social and leadership skills are developed and guidance is available for both education and academic issues.

≡ Looking Ahead members attend a special movie screening in Los Angeles. *The Actors Fund Archives.*

≡ The Looking Ahead Leadership Council gathers in Los Angeles. *The Actors Fund Archives.*

≡ Members of the Los Angeles–based Looking Ahead program tour the University of Southern California's campus. *The Actors Fund Archives.*

Housing

In the 1990s, The Actors Fund started addressing the need for affordable, supportive, and special needs housing. The Aurora, Palm View, and Schermerhorn are three examples of how The Fund has responded.

The Aurora

In 1996, as housing costs skyrocketed, The Actors Fund addressed the growing need for affordable housing by opening the Aurora, a 178-unit apartment building on Fifty-seventh Street in New York City. The Aurora provides housing and support services to working entertainment professionals, seniors, and persons with AIDS.

≡ The welcoming Palm View Residence serves Actors Fund clients in Southern California. *The Actors Fund Archives.*

≡ The thirty-story Aurora on Fifty-seventh Street and Tenth Avenue in New York City. *The Actors Fund Archives.*

Originally built as a luxury condominium, the Aurora sat empty for seven years after its developer went bankrupt. Purchased and renovated with thirty-four million dollars in federal low-income tax credits, the Aurora was completed through a partnership with Housing and Services Incorporated, a nonprofit housing developer and the Related Company as the tax credit syndicator.

The Actors Fund then hired Common Ground Community as property manager and staffed the building with a social service and activities program. Visiting Nurse Services provided the homecare services for residents in need, and a vibrant community began to form. A theater desk was set up for donated tickets, and a resident newsletter was created. A full activities program was launched for the 120 disabled or retired residents with more than 70 percent of the activities led by either residents or volunteers.

The Palm View Residence

In 1998, the Palm View Residence opened in Southern California. Through a partnership with the West Hollywood Community Housing Corporation, Palm View, an attractive forty-unit garden apartment complex for low-income persons with AIDS, was opened with thirty-five of the forty units designated for those from the entertainment community.

≡ The Schermerhorn House will expand The Fund's housing and services into Brooklyn, New York, via this residential building that will include performance space and on-site social services.

Schermerhorn

Continuing this tradition of supportive housing, The Schermerhorn House will open in Brooklyn, New York, in 2008. The Fund joined forces with Common Ground to construct a residential building that will include more than two hundred affordable, permanent low-income apartments for single adults.

Acknowledgments

The rich and developing history represented in this book cannot adequately recognize all of those who are part of The Actors Fund family. The generosity and talent of so many have made it possible to provide necessary programs and services to ALL performing arts and entertainment professionals. We are honored to rely on our corporate and institutional friends and entertainment industry unions, as well as the ongoing support of the Edwin Forrest Society, our In The Spotlight donors and our loyal Membership support.

As we look forward to our next 125 years, we pause to acknowledge those who work tirelessly each day to fulfill the mission of The Actors Fund. This book is dedicated to them.

The Actors Fund Board of Trustees

(as of July 1, 2008)

Brian Stokes Mitchell, *President*
Charles Hollerith, Jr., *Secretary*
John A. Duncan, Jr., *Treasurer*
Philip J. Smith, *1st Vice President*
Lynn Redgrave, *2nd Vice President*
Bebe Neuwirth, *3rd Vice President*
Philip S. Birsh, *4th Vice President*

Joseph P. Benincasa, *Executive Director*

Alec Baldwin
Jed W. Bernstein
Jeffrey Bolton
John Breglio
J. Nicholas Counter, III
Nancy Coyne
Misha Dabich
Merle Debuskey
Rick Elice
John Erman
Joyce Gordon
Marc Grodman, M.D.
John C. Hall, Jr.
Anita Jaffe
Kate Edelman Johnson
Steve Kalafer

Michael Kerker
Rocco Landesman
Stewart F. Lane
Alan Levey
Paul Libin
Kristen Madsen
Kevin McCollum
Audra McDonald
Mike Mearian
Katharine Minehart
James L. Nederlander
Martha Nelson
Phyllis Newman
Jack O'Brien
Dale C. Olson
A.J. Pocock
Jane Powell
Harold Prince
Abby Schroeder
Thomas C. Short
David Steiner
Edward D. Turen
Tom Viola
Honey Waldman
Jomarie Ward
Scott Weiner
Joseph H. Wender
B.D. Wong
Mark Zimmerman
George Zuber

The Actors Fund Staff

(as of July 1, 2008)

National Headquarters

Joseph P. Benincasa, *Executive Director*
Barbara Davis, L.M.S.W., *Chief Program Officer*
Ina Sorens Clark, *Chief Development Officer*
Anthony Lopez-Linus, *Chief Financial Officer*
Paul Riedel, *Executive Assistant*

Development/Communication

Suzanne Tobak, *Director of Advancement & Special Projects*
Louie Anchondo, *Director of Special Events*
DJ Brumfield, *Director of Institutional Giving*
Judith Fish, *Director of Individual Giving*
Wally Munro, *Director of Planned Giving*
David Engelman, *Manager, Special Events*
Celia Gannon, *Manager, Special Projects*
Megan Quinn, *Manager, Major Gifts*
Harry Ballard, *Membership Assistant*
Jose Delgado, *Membership Associate*
David Gusty, *Major Gifts Associate*
Jay Haddad, *Membership Assistant*
Amy Picar, *Special Events Assistant*
Timothy Pinckney, *Producer/Staff Writer*
Tina Benanav, *Communications and Design Associate*
Daniel Scholz, *Internet Communications Associate*

Finance & Administration

Connie Yoo, *Corporate Controller*
Erica Chung, *Accounts Payable Supervisor*
Carlos de Jesus, *Manager, Accounting*
Jian Bing Ho, *Senior Accountant*
Zehava Krinsky, *Accountant*
Victor Mendoza, *Senior Accountant*
Joy Pascua-Kim, *Executive Assistant*
John Sol, *Account Payable Clerk*

Human Resources & Administration

Carol Wilson, *Director of Human Resources*
Camille Codner, *Receptionist/Office Manager*
Charlene Morgan, *Employee Benefits Manager*
Manira Hossain, *Human Resources Assistant*

Information Technology

Israel Duran, *Director of Information Technology*
Jeff Woo, *Network Administrator*
Ricardo (Rick) Montero, *IT Help Desk/PC Technician*

Social Services – Eastern Region

Tamar Shapiro, L.C.S.W., *Director of Social Services, National*
Stephanie Linwood-Coleman, L.C.S.W., *Supervisor of Services Seniors & the Disabled*
Dale Daley, L.C.S.W., *Supervisor of the Entertainment Assistance Program, Eastern Region*
Carol Harris-Mannes, L.C.S.W., *Phyllis Newman Women's Health Initiative*
Lucy Seligson, L.M.S.W., *Intake Social Worker/Housing Specialist*
Kenton Curtis, *Supervisor of HIV/AIDS Initiative, Eastern Region*
Elizabeth Avedon, L.C.S.W., *HIV/AIDS Initiative*
Marjorie Roop, L.C.S.W., *HIV/AIDS Initiative*
Robert Rosenthal, L.C.S.W., *HIV/AIDS Initiative*
Rosalyn Gilbert, L.C.S.W., *Supervisor of Chemical Dependency Services*
Lynell Herzer, M.S.W., *Chemical Dependence Services*
Amanda Clayman, L.M.S.W., *Entertainment Assistance Program*
Thomas Lorio, L.M.S.W., *HIV/AIDS Initiative*
Alice Vienneau, M.S.W., *The Dancers' Resource*
Gloria Jones, *Administrative Coordinator*
Dalin Rivera, *Data Assistant*
Samuel A. Smith, *Data Control Supervisor*

Health Insurance Resource Center

James Brown, *Director of Health Services, National*
Renata Marinaro, M.S.W., *Manager, Special Projects*
Elizabeth Tripp, *Administrative Coordinator*

The Actors Work Program NY

Katherine Schrier, *Director of Actors Work Program, National*
Icem Benamu, *A.T.E.P. Counselor*
Billie Levinson, *Office Coordinator/Job Developer*
Ell Miocene, *Career Counselor*

Richard Renner, *Education Coordinator*
Patricia Schwadron, *Career Counselor Supervisor*

Al Hirschfeld Free Health Clinic
Jim Spears, M.D., *Medical Director*
Janet Pearl, *Health Services Manager*
Ruth Shin, *Administrative Coordinator*

The Aurora

Social Services
Ellen Celnik, L.M.S.W., *Director of Housing
    Program Services*
Lorriane Chisholm, *Receptionist*
John Barrow, L.C.S.W., *Social Worker*
Hope Geteles, L.M.S.W., *Social Worker*
Elizabeth Lawlor, *Office Manager*
Jonathan Margolies, L.C.S.W., *Associate Director*
Thomas Pileggi, *Activities Coordinator*
Linda Sax Craig, *Senior Case Manager*

The Aurora Property Management Office

Seymour Hunter, *Rent Coordinator*
Keisha Gardner, *Office Manager*
Raymundo Lizarraga, *Superintendent*
Claudette McCee, *Tenant & Intake Service
    Coordinator*
Raymond Peralta, *Security Supervisor*
Richard Pimentel, *Director of Property Management*
Derrick Sage, *Assistant Director*

Schermerhorn
Jamie Trachtenberg, *Associate Director*

Western Region
Keith McNutt, M.P.P., M.S.W, *Director of
    Western Region*

Development/Communication
David Michaels, *Director of Special Events*

Human Resources & Administration
Angelique Prahalis, *Office Administration Manager*
Stacy Renfroe, *Receptionist/Admin Assistant*

Social Services
Tina Abas, L.C.S.W., *Director of Social Services
    - Western Region*
Roni Blau, L.C.S.W., *Intake*
Russel Kieffer, L.C.S.W., *Supervisor, HIV/AIDS
    Initiative; Senior/Disability Programming*
Verdrie McCord, M.S.W., *HIV/AIDS Initiative*
Logan Speers, M.S.W., *Entertainment Assistance
    Program*
Michael Zaleski, M.S.W., *HIV/AIDS Initiative*
Linda Zimmerman, M.S.W., *HIV/AIDS Initiative*
Gabrielle Forman, L.C.S.W., *Seniors and the
    Disabled Services*
Gregory Polcyn, *Data Coordinator*

Health Insurance Resource Center
Daniel Kitowski, M.S.W., *Manager, HIRC,
    Western Region*
Aaron King, *Research Assistant*

The Actors Work Program LA
Michael Salerno, *Manager Actors Work Program,
    Western Region*
Joanne Webb, *A.T.E.P. Counselor*
Lauren Trotter, *Administrative Coordinator*

Looking Ahead Program
Heather Vanian, L.C.S.W., *Social Worker*
Laura Campbell, *Education Counselor*

Midwestern Region

Social Services
Donald Towne, L.C.S.W., *Director of Social Services
- Midwest Region*

The Actors Fund Homes

Administration and Management
Jordan Strohl, *Administrator*
Annmarie De Feis, *Administrative Manager*

Finance
Kim Eng, *Controller*

Human Resources
Jeanette Rivera, *Manager of Human Resources*

Nursing
Maria Box, *Director of Nursing*
Mandelia Williamson, *Nursing Supervisor*
Soo Donlin, *Nursing Supervisor*
Gendzyl Sosoban, *Clinical Supervisor*
Rose Thorne, *Staff Educator/Nursing Supervisor*

Recreation
Yalile Chavez, *Director of Recreation & Volunteers*

Social Services
Florence Lynch, *Director of Social Services*
Rochelle Nuss, *Admissions Coordinator/Social Worker*

Food Services
Cynthia Guest, *Director of Food Services*

Housekeeping & Laundry
Omar Castano, *Housekeeping Supervisor*

Maintenance & Security
Igor Denisenko, *Director of Maintenance & Security*